Tip-top

GARDENS

Great Britain's top 100 gardens

Veronica Mackinnon

foreword by Sarah Beeny

studio **cactus**

First published in Great Britain in 2004 by

studio **cactus** ltd

13 SOUTHGATE STREET WINCHESTER HAMPSHIRE SO23 9DZ
TEL 01962 878600 FAX 01962 859278
E-MAIL MAIL@STUDIOCACTUS.CO.UK WEBSITE WWW.STUDIOCACTUS.CO.UK

ISBN 1-904239-04-8

A catalogue record for this book is
available from the British Library.

Printed in Singapore by Imago

Contents

Foreword

Some of the happiest and most contented people I know are those who have beautiful gardens. But for anyone – even those who are not specially gifted in horticulture – there is nothing more pleasant than wandering around a lovely garden.

In this book Veronica Mackinnon describes the very best of the very best gardens in Britain, each one carefully selected for the particular delights it has to offer, and all open to the public to be enjoyed.

With land on our little island at a premium, any outside space is a luxury. Even the smallest garden can enhance your property, as well as bring you great pleasure, and the effects you can create are as diverse as your imagination allows.

So don't be tempted to neglect your garden and concentrate only on your interior design – take some inspiration from these pages and pop on your gardening gloves. You'll be amazed how rewarding it is!

Sarah Beeny

Property expert and TV presenter

Your own patch of paradise

So how do we set about creating our own little Shangri-la? There's no doubt that the best gardens are those that evolve slowly. The first thing is to live with your garden as it is for a while: all sorts of surprises may emerge through the seasons – spring bulbs in the wrong place, for example. And you need to work out where the sun stays longest, what type of soil you have and what space you need for the children. After that, however, comes the most important and enjoyable phase of planning your new garden: visiting as many gardens as you can, recording in a notebook all the plants and colour schemes you like, and photographing the pergola that takes your fancy.

Once you have the basic structure of your new garden in place, it's time to seek out those horticultural delicatessens, the garden nurseries. They grow top-quality plants, the staff will give you time and advice, and the choice is often far more interesting than at a local garden centre.

And then, once your garden is all planted up, you must make yet more visits to gardens. Seek out the gardener or owner and ask how he or she trains that rambling rose, what mulch is used, and when the dahlias are lifted. Pick as many brains as you can, take the information home and apply it. It's vital you visit a local garden at different times of the year to glean ideas on how to keep your plot looking good from one season to the next. But, most importantly, just keep on visiting gardens – it makes for a great day out!

Nicholas Tripp

Garden consultant and designer

Author's introduction

You might suppose that writing this book has been a pleasure. Well, the research was certainly blissful. Visiting gardens is always a joy and one generally comes away from a garden at most dazzled by the magnificent planting or inspired by the sculptures, and at least content, full of tea and cake, and clutching a postcard for granny and a new plant for that awkward corner.

Yet this author is not happy. Selecting 100 gardens for inclusion in the guide has been torture. The agonizing was not about the gardens that have been included within these pages, for I know that they fully deserve their place, but about the fact that I had to omit so many excellent gardens, both public and private. This will undoubtedly lose me numerous friends, and to them I must apologize unreservedly. It is not that these gardens weren't good enough to 'get in'; it is simply that I decided the only way to compile a condensed guide such as this was to set and strictly adhere to certain criteria.

The first of these was that the garden must be open to the public regularly. This immediately excludes that vast slice of horticultural heaven, the private gardens that open for charity once or twice a year under the National Gardens Scheme. Many are unsurpassed, and almost all are excellent. Furthermore, there are many other historic, important or just beautiful gardens that are in private hands and whose owners are kind enough to allow access to groups and enthusiasts by appointment. Generally these too have not qualified, but to them I raise my glass, for it is a huge invasion of privacy when that coach turns up and we all troop in, muttering criticisms or compliments.

Next, I had to cover all four corners of England, Scotland and Wales – yet I could have compiled a guide called, for example, *The Top 100 Gardens of Gloucestershire*, and still have had some to spare.

My third criterion, however, was that each garden should represent excellence in its field: topiary at Levens Hall, woodland planting at the Savill and Valley Gardens, or roses at Mottisfont, for example. Some simply sublime gardens, such as Hidcote and Sissinghurst, are of course superlative on all levels.

Finally, do remember as you walk round these gardens that the man shovelling manure onto the roses in the pouring rain would really appreciate a smile and a kind comment about how beautiful it all looks. He is as likely to be the owner-duke as the under-gardener – either way, gardens do not happen by accident. They are the result of many days, months, years and sometimes centuries of planning, hard labour and passion, and those involved deserve huge recognition and credit. I take my hat off to them all, past, present and, I trust, future.

Veronica Mackinnon

Contact us at:

studio cactus ltd

13 SOUTHGATE STREET WINCHESTER HAMPSHIRE SO23 9DZ
E-MAIL: MAIL@STUDIOCACTUS.CO.UK
www.tiptopguides.co.uk

Gardens – a potted history

How gardens came to Britain

3000 to 1500 BC – The Egyptians, Persians and Assyrians created the first enclosed 'gardens' as shady refuges from the sun and as safe enclosures against marauding wild animals. Over time, these gardens became more sophisticated, growing a wide variety of plants for food, religious significance, colour and scent, and featuring canals and water features, raised pathways and ornamental trees. The word 'paradise' has its origins in the name that the Persians gave to these gardens.

1500 BC to the birth of Christ: Greeks travelling in Asia took Islamic 'paradise gardens' home with them. In time, their influence spread across the Roman empire.

43 to 400 AD – Romans occupying Britain grew vines and other imported plants, including Mediterranean herbs.

500 to 1000 AD – Christianity spreads, leading to the building of monasteries. Monastic gardens grew herbs and medicinal plants, as well as food crops and vines.

1000 to 1500 AD – Noblemen, physicians and other wealthy individuals planted their own gardens. Initially shady, grassy plots, these developed into the medieval 'flowery mead', characterized by fragrant plants, raised beds, bower seats and areas of turf (our first lawns, perhaps), often arranged around a central water feature. Floriferous but structured, enclosed and formal in style, these 'flowery meads' were our first truly ornamental gardens.

Gardens of the Tudors and Stuarts

In Britain, by the 16th century, the Tudors were creating gardens with plant material brought back from all over Europe, the Ottoman empire and the newly discovered Americas. Features such as knot gardens and labyrinths appeared, and gardens became bigger but remained formal in style and enclosed by walls or hedges.

During the reign of the Stuarts in the 17th century, James I and other enthusiasts continued to encourage British gardeners and plant collectors such as the two John Tradescants (father and son) on their travels to Europe, Africa and the Americas. After the Civil War, and with closer political relationships established with the Continent, French, Italian and Dutch influences began to take hold in Britain. With the introduction of long canals, straight avenues of trees disappearing to the far horizons, and vast parterres, gardens were still formal and symmetrical but were opened up to the surrounding countryside.

Tulip mania

By the early 1600s tulips had spread from the Ottoman empire through Europe to the Netherlands. This austere country, with its flat lands and grey weather, had been at war with Spain, and the people were desperate for a little colour in their lives. As the war ended, and a flourishing trade in textiles and diamonds brought new houses and gardens, tulips became objects of desire and began to sell for large sums

of money. The most popular blooms were 'broken' or striped (bulbs that were, we now know, affected by a virus). The bulbs were out of the ground and available for sale only from June to November. Thus dealers began to trade while the tulips were still in the ground, bulbs often changing hands many times before they were lifted. As prices soared, single bulbs sold at auction for sums equivalent to several years' income for a merchant. In 1637, however, as a result of suspicion and concern about the inflated prices, one auction attracted no bids. Panic set in and the market crashed, bankrupting many people. Luckily, the best growers continued to cultivate tulip bulbs, and in time added other bulbs to their list – hyacinths, daffodils, lilies, and many, many more. The Netherlands remains one of the top bulb producers in the world today.

The 18th-century English Landscape Garden

With the advent of the Grand Tour (when every wealthy young man was despatched to travel around Europe to study art and literature), the romance of the Italian classical landscape, with its wooded hills and waterfalls, became hugely popular with the landed gentry. William Kent and Lancelot 'Capability' Brown are perhaps the best-known of the designers who interpreted this style into what is now known as the English Landscape Garden. These stylized, naturalistic parklands often included artificial lakes, cascades, temples, bridges and grottoes. Apparently unfenced, they blended into the distant countryside, with woodland and copses carefully arranged to enhance the scene.

Many of Britain's great houses have examples of such idealistic landscapes – 'Capability' Brown's include Alnwick Castle, Chatsworth (see pages 122–123), Harewood House, Longleat, Blenheim Palace, Highclere Castle, Petworth and Castle Ashby. It also has to be said, however, that this fashion and its exponents were undoubtedly responsible for the destruction of a great number of magnificent formal gardens.

The 19th century

Humphry Repton modified the English Landscape style by re-introducing terraces, flower gardens and pleasure grounds in which to walk. Repton also championed the cause of smaller, more accessible

Longleat is a typical example of the work of 'Capability' Brown. He carefully planned and planted the surrounding countryside to make it part of the 'garden'.

gardens, as did John Claudius Loudon. These ideas were often adopted by the middle classes, who as a result of the Industrial Revolution had made reasonable fortunes and built new houses in the fashionable Gothic style. Curiosities such as monkey puzzle trees were greatly sought after, and eclectic collections of specimens were randomly planted into lawns and surrounded by beds filled with garish bedding plants. This style became known as the Gardenesque. One of the most impressive bedding schemes can be found in the parterre at Waddesden Manor, Buckinghamshire (*see* page 46).

Rock gardens became the height of fashion and were constructed on an unimaginable scale, imitations of Japanese gardens were built, and woodland gardens accommodated the fashionable new plants brought home from China and the Himalayas. Plant collectors of the 19th century included Robert Fortune, Joseph Hooker, Ernest H Wilson, George Forest, and Frank Kingdon-Ward.

William Robinson encouraged a more natural style, which included blocks of different plants within large planted areas (our first herbaceous borders) and wild flowers grown in long grass – a very naturalistic concept for the stiff Victorian era.

The 20th century

The past 100 years have seen many changes in the style of gardens. At the start of the 20th century the Arts and Crafts movement was under way: gardens were laid out in a formal structured style but were cloaked in loose and naturalistic planting, following the style created by Gertrude Jekyll (*see* page 14). Rodmarton Manor, in Gloucestershire, is an excellent example of the Arts and Crafts garden. This influence also manifested itself in Lawrence Johnston's garden at Hidcote Manor (*see* page 37) and later at Sissinghurst, created by Vita Sackville-West and Harold Nicolson (*see* pages 60–61).

Many 20th-century garden creators – Harold Peto and Clough Williams-Ellis to name but two – drew their inspiration from Renaissance Italy. Harold Peto's home at Iford Manor, Wiltshire (*see* pages 74–75), is one of the finest 20th-century Italianate gardens.

The Modern Movement, with its functional, simplistic design, emerged between the two world wars. After World War II, when there was so much rebuilding going on and the large, high-maintenance garden was in decline, smaller, post-modern gardens became commonplace, demonstrating the transatlantic influence of Roberto Burle Marx and Thomas Church.

The latter part of the 20th century produced many top British designers, some of whom have already earned their places in the garden history books: Sylvia Crowe, Russell Page, Geoffrey Jellicoe, John Brookes, David Hicks, Arabella Lennox-Boyd, Charles Jencks, Roy Strong, Bunny Guinness and many more. Patrons who have allowed their designers to experiment must also be applauded, none more so than HRH The Prince of Wales, who continues to embellish his innovative and interesting garden at Highgrove, in Gloucestershire, with new ideas.

Yet it is impossible to label the gardens of the past few decades with any one definitive style. It would appear that, rather like clothes, almost anything goes.

Gertrude Jekyll (1843–1932)

The most influential garden designer of the 20th century was Gertrude Jekyll. Having turned to gardening late in life, she worked from the 1890s through to the 1930s, teaming up for part of her career with Edwin Lutyens, a young Arts and Crafts architect of renown. Where Lutyens designed the houses and hard-works (paths, raised beds and walls dividing the garden into 'rooms'), Jekyll softened the formal lines with informal, naturalistic planting, planned in harmonious colour schemes. Jekyll's love of plants and nature played a large part in the style she adopted. Furthermore, her

Gertrude Jekyll's cottage-garden style of planting remains immensely popular today.

very poor sight and art school training gave her a 'watercolour wash' view of the gardens she created, especially the herbaceous borders for which she became so famous. Jekyll was much sought after and designed some 350 gardens. Her influence persists today.

Jekyll gardens to visit include: Barrington Court, Ilminster, Somerset TA19 0NQ, Tel 01460 241938; Folly Farm, Sulhamstead, Reading, Berkshire RG7 4DF, Tel 01635 841541; Hestercombe Gardens, Cheddon Fitzpaine, Taunton, Somerset TA2 8LG, Tel 01823 413923; and The Manor House, Upton Grey (see page 69). Munstead Wood, Godalming, Surrey, was Jekyll's home for nearly 30 years and, like other Jekyll gardens, is open through the National Gardens Scheme (Yellow Book, Tel 01483 211535).

Gardens – the future

As a result of enormous media interest in gardening, not least on television, every house-owner, however small the property, is now aware that designing and building a garden is affordable and achievable. An amazing range of plants, garden equipment, tools, containers, ready-planted hanging baskets, water features (as well as totally unrelated miscellany) can be purchased from the garden centres that have sprung up nationwide. We now have the horticultural equivalent of fast-food and supermarket chains.

But one thing remains certain: the gardens that have stood the test of time – some of them for many centuries – are those that were well thought-out (whether designed by amateurs or professionals), constructed with good-quality, durable materials, and planted with carefully sourced, well-grown, befitting plants. And I predict that this will continue to be the case in the future.

Symbols used in this book

Plants for sale

Shop

Tea room

Toilet facilities

Unlicensed restaurant

Licensed restaurant

Garden suitable in part for wheelchair users

Dogs welcome but must be on a lead at all times

Coaches welcome but we advise you to phone ahead

Opening times may vary, so we strongly advise you to phone before planning a visit

"...I have broken my back, my finger nails and sometimes my heart..."

Vita Sackville-West, 1958

Southern England

East Ruston Old Vicarage

East Ruston, Norwich, Norfolk NR12 9HN Tel 01692 650432
Apr–Oct, Wed, Fri–Sun & BH 2–5.30

www.e-ruston-oldvicaragegardens.co.uk

Any student of garden design should visit East Ruston Old Vicarage to observe good design theory put into practice. A backbone of structure runs throughout with topiary, hedges, avenues and arches dividing the garden into a series of rooms and rides. There are innovative garden buildings, walls and pergolas.

The lines of the formal ponds are crisp and modern, and there are a couple of wacky sculptures. Few gardens borrow focal

points from the surrounding landscape as skilfully as East Ruston does: the gardens frame the church and a lighthouse on the coast beyond. But the greatest surprise of this garden is the

If you have ever felt the northeast wind on a January day in Norfolk you will be amazed that any plant survives the winter at East

plants. Proximity to the sea and broad shelterbelts of pines have enabled Alan Gray and Graham Robeson the garden's creators, to grow an extraordinary range of plants from all corners of the globe, many of which we would consider too tender for Cornwall, never mind north Norfolk. Agaves and tree ferns abound, with echeverias and cannas jostling for space amongst aeoniums, cacti and palms. The garden is crammed with interesting species, but this is certainly not to the cost of the overall effect.

East Ruston is, quite simply, stunning. There are many styles of planting within the garden: don't miss the Californian border and Desert Wash, with its drifts of eschscholzias and exclamation marks of aloes. There are some long borders, the Dutch garden, a wild garden and more. Even the window boxes stop you in your tracks, and countless pots, urns and other containers are crammed with the weird, the wonderful and the colourful.

East Ruston is a modern-day Hidcote: a garden of great merit and a top-class example of expert plantsmanship and design – definitely worth a lengthy detour.

Ruston. This garden should encourage us all to experiment more with plants that are considered tender.

19

Blickling Hall

Aylsham, Norwich, Norfolk NR11 6NF Tel 01263 738030
Apr–Oct, Wed–Sun (also Tue in Aug) 10.15–5.15; Nov–Dec, Thu–Sun 11–4; Jan–Mar, Sat–Sun 11–4

www.nationaltrust.org.uk

Two vast, ancient yew hedges flank the approach to this fine brick-built Jacobean mansion. To the east lies a large parterre with yew topiary and raised walkways from which to admire the geometric shapes. During the 1930s designer Norah Lindsay instated the planting scheme that you see here today. The Doric temple beyond the parterre is surrounded by azaleas, and the woods are vivid with bluebells. The neoclassical orangery houses tender, shade-loving plants, and there is a secret garden that is remarkable if only for its simplicity. In the west garden you'll find magnolias, hostas and climbing roses. The lake and parkland are home to many birds, including water fowl and the elusive bittern.

Felbrigg Hall, near Cromer, has an immaculate walled garden with box hedges, flower borders and vegetable beds (tel 01263 837444).

Wyken Hall

Stanton, Bury St Edmunds, Suffolk IP31 2DW Tel 01359 250287
Apr–Sep, Sun–Fri 2–6

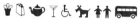

www.gardens-guide.com

After the wonderful café and treasure-trove shop at Wyken's entrance, your next discovery will be the charming cottage garden, where traditional planting froths over a little gothic-style cottage. At the entrance to the Suffolk-pink Elizabethan hall there is a quincunx of box circles with a small, central fountain. After an encounter with the peacocks, move through the edible garden into the orchard and well-stocked kitchen garden. Passing the red-hot border, you enter a series of hedged rooms, designed by Arabella

Lennox-Boyd, incorporating rose, herb and knot gardens. Through the blue gate lies a wildlife pond with seats on a deck – a perfect place to rest. Wyken Hall is romantic and charming – a joy.

The shop sells wines produced in Wyken Hall's vineyards. There is also a farmers' market every Saturday 9–1.

Helmingham Hall Gardens

Stowmarket, Suffolk 1P14 6EF Tel 01473 890363

May to mid-Sep, Sun 2–6; Wed pm by appointment

www.members.aol.com/helmingest

The two drawbridges over the wide moat encircling Helmingham Hall are raised each night and lowered every morning, as they have been by the Tollemache family for some 19 generations over the 500 years for which the Hall has been standing. The brick-built house is surrounded by 160ha (400 acres) of parkland, populated by red and fallow deer and home to many ancient oaks.

The walled garden dates back further than the hall, to Saxon times, and the original moat can be seen beyond the 18th-century walls. Between the two moats lies the parterre, patterned with

I was lucky enough to chat to the head gardener who has worked for Lord Tollemache for nearly 50 years. He has immense

neat yew domes, box hedges and attractive bedding schemes. Surrounding the parterre is the hybrid musk rose garden with underplanting of London pride.

The beautifully designed double herbaceous borders cross the walled garden, dividing it into four sections. Muted colours complement the roses early in the season, giving way to hotter colours later on. Other attractions include a shrub border, the annual border, the spring border and the grass border. You'll also find a tunnel dripping with ornamental gourds, and enviable rows of vegetables.

The orchard and wild garden are beyond the walls, and to the east of the house lie the knot and rose gardens, which were created in the 1980s. These adjoin the old coach house, where you can enjoy delicious cream teas.

Helmingham has a particular grace and presence, and while the gardens are not enormous, they have a great sense of place as well as a delightfully intimate atmosphere.

charm and wisdom: long may he (and his ilk) continue to pass on their encyclopaedic knowledge to the next generation.

23

Audley End

Saffron Walden, Essex CB11 4JF Tel 01799 522842
Apr–Sep, Wed–Sun & BH 11–6 (last entry 5); Oct, Sat–Sun 11–5 (last entry 4)

www.english-heritage.org.uk

The imposing 17th-century, Jacobean mansion stands in peaceful lawns overlooking a mirror-calm lake. The huge formal gardens that originally surrounded the house were reshaped by 'Capability' Brown in the mid-18th century with landscaped parkland, a serpentine lake, Robert Adam temples, bridges, monuments and vistas. The intricate Victorian parterre has 170 geometrically designed beds filled with vibrantly coloured perennials, roses and lilies, surrounding a central fountain. The 19th-century Pond Garden has an attractive square pool and is encircled by climbing roses.

Beyond lies the organic kitchen garden, stocked with old varieties of fruit trees, vegetables and herbs. Audley End is a great day out, and I recommend it for a relaxing walk and a family picnic.

Don't miss the gardener's bothy in the kitchen garden (restored by English Heritage and the Henry Doubleday Research Association).

The Beth Chatto Gardens

Elmstead Market, Colchester, Essex CO7 7DB Tel 01206 822007
Mar–Oct, Mon–Sat 9–5; Nov–Feb, Mon–Fri 9–4

www.bethchatto.co.uk

Beth Chatto has spent over 40 years transforming a piece of wasteland into one of Britain's leading gardens. The metamorphosis of this brambly corner of a fruit farm is extraordinary. Beth has extracted the land's full potential by working in tandem with the adverse conditions. Schemes range from the famous dry gravel garden to bogs, ponds, woodland shade and scree beds. Mrs Chatto has an exceptional eye for colour and form, and is a remarkable plantswoman. At every interval

you'll stop to exclaim over unusual and attractive colour combinations, leaf textures and perennial rarities. Her garden illustrates that there are plants for every difficult corner and for all types of soil.

Visiting the nursery is an education in itself. You can buy many rare or unusual plants, and they are well grown and of excellent quality.

Anglesey Abbey

Lode, Cambridge CB5 9EJ Tel 01223 811200

Apr–Oct, Wed–Sun & BH Mon 10.30–5.30 (also Jul–Aug, daily, Thu to 8); Nov–Mar, Wed–Sun, 10.30–4

www.nationaltrust.org.uk/angleseyabbey

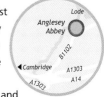

The remains of a 12th-century priory exist within the structure of the 16th-century house, but the gardens at Anglesey Abbey are much younger – the creation of the 1st Lord Fairhaven in the mid-1900s.

The 14ha (35 acres) of trees, lawns, avenues and hedged enclosures might appear plain if they were not graced by a collection of extraordinary sculptures and historic statuary: Roman gods and emperors; French bronzes; a plethora of statues from Stowe; marble urns, columns, sundials and satyrs. All are placed strategically to guide the eye and delight those who wander through these remarkable pleasure grounds. The gardens are attractive and colourful: the Herbaceous Garden is beautifully planted and the Dahlia Garden radiates brilliant hues in late summer. There is a winter garden and acres of bulbs to enjoy in the spring.

It is worth buying the guide book to obtain maximum informatio about the history and origins of the statues and sculptures.

Cottesbrooke Hall

Cottesbrooke, Northampton NN6 8PF Tel 01604 505808
May–Jun, Wed–Thu & BH 2–5; Jul–Sep, Thu & BH 2–5.30

www.cottesbrookehall.co.uk

The attractive 18th-century house stands in fine landscaped parkland encircled by the prettiest of Northamptonshire countryside. The gardens are largely a 20th-century creation; Geoffrey Jellicoe and Sylvia Crowe both had a hand in the terrace by the south front of the house, which commands views towards Brixworth

Church, a large 7th-century building. The house is flanked by courtyards and enclosures filled with colourful planting, ponds and statuary. The Monkey Pond is a charming water feature within a shady sunken terrace. The herbaceous borders are sumptuous, and the 18th-century figures in the Statue Walk are particularly impressive.

The house (open as garden) holds fine furniture and porcelain as well as the famous Woolavington Collection of sporting pictures.

Coton Manor

Guilsborough, Northamptonshire NN6 8RQ Tel 01604 740219

Apr–Sep, Tue–Sat & BH noon–5.30 (also Apr–May, Sun)

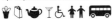

www.cotonmanor.co.uk

Ian and Susie Pasley-Tyler have built on Ian's parents' and grandparents' layout to create the most floriferous garden I have visited. The stone house is swathed with roses and wisteria, the terraces are crammed with pots of plenty, the rose garden is a sheltered formal space, with pink-and-white scented varieties set off by grey *Stachys byzantina*. The woodland and water gardens have many unusual perennials and bulbs, and the main pond adds a peaceful element. Otherwise, there are borders, filled to the brim with the rare and unusual to amaze even the experts and

carefully colour-controlled or designed to look their best at a particular time of year. As if this is not enough, there is a herb garden, a wildflower meadow, an orchard and bluebell woods.

The spectacular pink rose climbing into a tree, known as 'Gardener' Pink' but not truly identified, may be on sale in the top-class nursery

The Old Rectory Gardens

Sudborough, Northamptonshire NN14 3BX Tel 01832 733247

Apr–Jun, Tue & Sat 10–4; Jul–Sep, Sat 10–4

www.oldrectorygardens.co.uk

The 0.8ha (2 acres) surrounding the well-proportioned Georgian rectory have been developed over 20 years by the owners, Mr and Mrs Huntington, and garden designer Rupert Golby. By the front door are shade-tolerant plants, including some interesting shrubs. On the south side of the house, the central lawn is surrounded by a circle of scented roses with luxurious under-planting of alliums, purple sage and lavender; the elegant white border; a bed of contrasting evergreens; a shrub border;

and a magnificent herbaceous scheme. The pond is a delight in spring with massed hellebores, and the potager, designed by the late Rosemary Verey, is both decorative and productive.

Note *Ilex crenata* 'Convexa' in the potager, used as an alternative to box edging. In recent years 'box blight' has been eradicating box.

29

Coughton Court

Alcester, Warwickshire B49 5JA Tel 01789 762435

Apr–Sep, Wed–Sun & BH 11–5.30 (also Tue in Jul–Aug); Oct, Sat–Sun 11–5.30

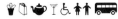

www.coughtoncourt.co.uk

Coughton Court is an impressive, attractive 15th-century house, filled with pictures and objets d'art, many of great historical merit. The fine gardens have been created and enhanced since 1992 by Clare Throckmorton and her daughter Christina Williams. The walled

garden has enormous herbaceous borders, one planted with hot colours and the other with softer hues. The rose labyrinth is voluptuous and imaginative, while the White Garden offers cool serenity. The bog garden veers towards the wild rather than manicured, and there are good riverside walks. The formal garden and courtyard are breathtaking.

Inspired by his own garden, Claude Monet (1840–1926) famously said "More than anything I must must have flowers, always, always…".

Ryton Organic Gardens

Coventry CV8 3LG Tel 02476 303517
Gardens open daily 9–5, except Christmas week

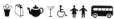

www.hdra.org.uk

The home of the Henry Doubleday Research Association, the largest organic organization in Europe, this is not only an aesthetically pleasing garden, but a fascinating centre of education and information. 'Organic' has been defined as 'recognizing the whole environment

in which plants grow…and that all living things are inter-related and interdependent.' Forget noxious sprays and chemical fertilizers; think ladybirds and compost heaps. But you do not need to be a crank – or even a gardener – to enjoy Ryton. The many small gardens are carefully designed, informative, and

diverse in planting and style, and the Vegetable Kingdom is an experience not to be missed (save it for rainy moments). Ryton answers all your horticultural problems, and there's an excellent shop.

There are herb gardens, orchards, soft fruit, vegetable and flower gardens to inspire you with ideas, whatever size your plot.

Upton House

Banbury, Oxfordshire OX15 6HT Tel 01295 670266

Apr– Oct, Mon–Wed noon–5, Sat–Sun & BH 11–5; Nov–Dec, Sat–Sun noon–4

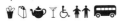

www.nationaltrust.org.uk

A422

Upton House

Banbury ▼

There can be few more handsome houses than Upton, with its long, tree-lined drive ending in the hedged entrance courtyard. Rose-clad terraces lead down to a wide lawn terminating in a ha-ha framed by huge conifers. But the surprise lies beyond the lawn-edge. There is a hidden valley below, whose terraces burst with colour. There are rose gardens, dry plantings, shrubberies, the National Collection of Asters, a kitchen garden and

beautiful herbaceous borders sweeping down to a lake in the valley floor. You can zig-zag down the terraces and follow the lawns to the west side of the house, where you'll find an informal water garden.

The house contains a staggering collection of paintings, including works by Tintoretto, Stubbs, Bosch, El Greco and Holbein.

Bryan's Ground

Stapleton, Near Presteigne, Herefordshire LD8 2LP Tel 01544 260001
Apr–Aug, Sun–Mon 2–5

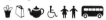

www.hortus.co.uk

Bryan's Ground is a remarkable garden created by two gifted men: David Wheeler, garden writer and publisher of the quarterly *Hortus* (a must for every connoisseur), and Simon Dorrell, painter and garden designer. There are the vistas and focal points; calm canals and vibrant planting; vast drifts of *Iris sibirica*; a 'green theatre', and paths so swamped by ebullient planting that it is hard to find a route through. Simon and David have a sense

of humour and a theatrical edge: bed springs and chains decorate pergolas and statues, rusting sheets of corrugated iron are stylishly used as fencing material, and classical music wafts on the air from the greenhouse. Bryan's Ground is modern, wacky, fun, pretty: an inventive garden with a classical accent.

Nothing is thrown away at Bryan's Ground – you will find many splendid ideas on re-using all sorts of household bits and pieces!

Hampton Court Gardens

Near Hope under Dinmore, Leominster, Herefordshire HR6 0PN Tel 01568 797777
Tue–Sun & BH Mon 11–5

      www.hamptoncourt.org.uk

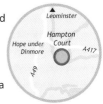

Hampton Court is the sort of castle you would expect to find in fairytales of dragons, knights in armour and jousting contests. The castle dates back to the 15th century and, while it is not open to the public, forms a magical backdrop to the park and gardens.

After driving through the new gatehouse folly built by the American owners (it is they who have rescued Hampton Court from neglect and have commissioned the new gardens),

you enter the walled garden to find a utopia. The potager, swarming with cheerful gardeners on my visit, is not only productive but beautifully designed. Shining white

The shop stocks locally produced items of excellent quality, along with terracotta pots to die for. The standard of maintenance in

34

glasshouses, an orchard and borders burgeoning with heritage varieties of scrumptious salads and vegetables, provide supplies for the excellent shop and restaurant. Beyond lies designer Simon Dorrell's most inspired creation: the walled flower gardens.

The planting is indeed stunning, but what make this an exceptionally fine contemporary garden is the stepped canal running round two oak pavilions, and the Tudor-style patterning of the paths and beds.

There is more. This must be one of the few gardens where you actually walk behind a waterfall – this one tumbles into the pond in the sunken garden. There is a secret passage to the tower (find it yourselves...), a maze of a thousand yews in which to lose the children, and a 150-year-old wisteria tunnel. The Dutch Garden is simple and chic. The park and riverside walks are almost limitless, and you can enjoy your lunch in a Joseph Paxton orangery.

the gardens is superb, the staff are helpful and friendly. This is an example of a top-class product, and a visit is highly recommended.

The Lance Hattatt Design Garden

Near Weobley, Herefordshire HR4 8RN Tel 01544 318468
Apr–Oct, Wed 10–5

www.lancehattattdesign.co.uk

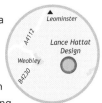

Designer Lance Hattatt has created a ravishing showpiece of contrasts, vistas and focal points. The many enclosures are filled with fascinating colours and planting, and you should try to visit at least twice, in different seasons, so as not to miss anything. Some schemes are restful and others striking – for example, the beds planted with silver cardoons and edged with

purple heucheras to mimic the copper beech nearby. Wild flowers, spring bulbs, old roses, topiary, a tower, rills, ponds and streams are all to be found in this contemporary garden designed in the best English tradition.

Courses, practical workshops and lectures are held here throughou the year. If you are interested, ask for a brochure.

Hidcote Manor Garden

Hidcote Bartrim, Chipping Campden, GL55 6LR Tel 01386 438333

Opening dates and times vary. Telephone for further information.

www.nationaltrust.org.uk

The unique garden at Hidcote was created by Lawrence Johnston in the early part of the 20th century, around a manor house set high in the hills above the Vale of Evesham. Johnston created sheltered, hedged rooms, passages and spaces of differing scale and intimacy filled with many and varied plants. In contrast to the closed-in rooms that brim with roses and lilies, there are large expanses of lawn and thrilling views over the valley below. You'll find winding paths by a woodland stream planted with

bog plants and flowering shrubs, borders filled with scorching red flowers, and a tiny space planted all in white. This is a place of genius, which everyone should visit.

Kiftsgate Court is nearby (tel 01386 43877). Do check the opening times of both gardens: Kiftsgate's differs from Hidcote's.

Bourton House

Bourton-on-the-Hill, Moreton-in-Marsh, Gloucestershire GL56 9AE Tel 01386 700754

Apr–Aug, Wed–Fri & BH Sun–Mon 10–5; Sep–Oct, Thu–Fri 10–5

🌱 🏠 🫖 ♿ 🚻 ♂♀ 🚌

www.bourtonhouse.com

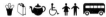

This is my idea of heaven. At the lower end of this picturesque Cotswold village stands a handsome, 18th-century stone house, with an exceptional tithe barn and cottages grouped around the courtyard. The gardens, surrounded by honey-coloured stone walls, are extremely well maintained. The lawns were humming with Dennis mowers on the day I visited – the best machines to make a sward look like a pair of green-striped, velvet pyjamas. My abiding memory of the gardens is box. Box hedges and topiary are used most imaginatively and structurally throughout: there are rope-twist edgings, twisted columns, pyramids, cones, balls and more, yet there is nothing severe or fussy about these gardens.

Owners Monique and Richard Paice have, over the past 20 years, created a wonderful garden. They have used an

Some 450m (500yd) down the road is the entrance to Sezincote, a wonderful contrast to Bourton House with its landscaped park

extraordinary range of plants in unusual combinations and breathtaking colour schemes, employing repetition to maintain unity and to link the different areas into a  cohesive whole. There is no visual jolt as you potter from the tropical borders to the knot garden, round woodland beds to the croquet lawn, through the shade tunnel (crammed with plants I had never seen before), to the seats offering matchless views over unspoilt acres of the fairest Gloucestershire countryside. There is a 3ha (7-acre) arboretum, a potager, a raised pond, a water garden, a series of luxuriant terraces and some deep herbaceous borders. Throughout the gardens you will notice an attention to detail in all facets of the design.

This is a garden to inspire, to admire and, most of all, to enjoy. It is very much a home, where the terriers eye you with suspicion and your hostess provides the most scrumptious teas. It has fired me with enthusiasm for my own garden, and I rate it in my top 10 in this book.

ndian-style architecture, vast trees and streamside gardens – don't miss it. Open Jan–Nov, Thu & Fri 2–6 or dusk (tel 01386 700444).

Sudeley Castle

Winchcombe, Cheltenham, Gloucestershire GL54 5JD Tel 01242 602308
Mar–Oct, daily 10.30–5.30

www.sudeleycastle.co.uk

This spectacular castle has a pedigree dating back a thousand years. The gardens have been sympathetically revamped by Lady Ashcombe and several notable designers. The stonework of the ruined tithe barn is a foil for climbers and flourishing perennials, and the ruins of a 15th-century banqueting hall are swathed with honeysuckle and rambling roses. In contrast, the Tudor knot garden with its clean lines, central fountain and Moorish-style mosaic dome has a contemporary feel. The Queens Garden

bursts with roses, and there's Mediterranean-style planting in the Secret Garden. Wild areas, a Victorian potager and a fine collection of buddleja make for a good day out.

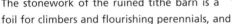

Oak trees that were mentioned in the _Domesday Book_ are still standing on the estate at Sudeley Castle.

The National Arboretum, Westonbirt

Westonbirt, Tetbury, Gloucestershire GL8 8QS Tel 01666 880220

Daily 10–5 (or dusk)

www.forestry.gov.uk/westonbirt

This is a mecca for tree enthusiasts. The Holford family began the planting of these 240ha (600 acres) in 1829, and many trees have now reached vast proportions. There are some 18,000 trees, from all over the temperate world, and the Forestry Commission

(which took over the arboretum in 1956) continues to add new specimens regularly. High points of the year are spring, when many trees and shrubs are in bloom, and autumn, which sees breathtaking colours, not least in the collection of spectacular Japanese maples. From mid-November to Christmas selected trees and paths are floodlit on weekend evenings, with magical results.

Westonbirt hosts the International Festival of Gardens, which offers opportunities for designers to show off their work on a more long-term basis than most other shows.

Find 100 varieties of roses in the delightful gardens at Hodges Barn in nearby Shipton Moyne – eight acres of beauty (tel 01666 88020).

Brook Cottage Garden

Well Lane, Alkerton, Banbury OX15 6NL Tel 01295 670303/670590

Easter Mon–Oct, Mon–Fri 9–6

www.visit-northoxfordshire.co.uk

Brook Cottage nestles into the side of a valley on the edge of Alkerton. Mrs Hodges and her late husband started to create the garden in the 1960s, taking advantage of the contours of the hillside by designing a succession of enclosed areas linked by winding

paths. Each compartment contains plants for the connoisseur, such as bog dwellers, shrub roses, unusual trees and bold clumps of architectural foliage. Every corner of the garden is jam-packed with flowers: a rainbow of bearded irises, alliums, nectaroscordums, regal pelargoniums and hundreds of

interesting perennials. The controlled profusion of clever planting is balanced by open spaces of lawn and glimpses of the Oxfordshire countryside. This well-loved garden is a joy to visit.

Brook Cottage is a home, where you put your entry money in the honesty box and make your own coffee from the kettle provided.

Chenies Manor Gardens

The Manor House, Chenies, Buckinghamshire WD3 6ER Tel 01494 762888
Apr–Oct, Wed–Thu & BH Mon 2–5

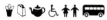

www.gardens-guide.com

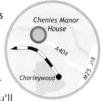

The main body of Chenies Manor dates from the 15th and 16th centuries. The entrance court is a cool green space with overhanging trees, shrubs and a central fountain. Passing through an arch, you enter the medieval-style flower gardens, where you'll encounter brimming borders around sunken lawns, pergolas, pleached trees and ancient outbuildings. In spring, the

courtyards are planted with massed tulips; in May these are lifted and replaced with vibrantly coloured dahlias, annuals and bedding plants. Beyond these there is the Physic Garden and White Garden. Surrounding the house are hot colours, which glow against the mellow brick. This is high-maintenance gardening, and the results are spectacular.

A blindfold pony used to pump up the village water supply from the medieval well located in the Physic Garden.

Cliveden Garden

Taplow, Maidenhead, Buckinghamshire SL6 0JA Tel 01628 605069
Mid-Mar to Oct, daily 11– 6; Nov–Dec 11–4

www.nationaltrust.org.uk

There are few houses today that still command such spectacular views over the Thames basin. In 1906 this 17th-century house became home to Nancy Astor, the first woman MP. Today the house is a top-class hotel, and the National Trust cares for the grounds. The Shell Fountain at the end of the Grand Avenue is particularly impressive. Hidden behind is the secluded Long Garden, a formal area of topiary and statues. There is a charming secret garden, a water garden and

glorious herbaceous planting near the house. The views over the parterre from the south front and from the Octagon Temple to the southwest are truly breathtaking.

Note the balustrade on the south front, carved in 1618–19 for the Villa Borghese in Rome and brought here by Lord Astor in 1896.

Stowe Landscape Gardens

Buckinghamshire MK1 5EH Tel 01280 822850
Mar–Oct, Wed–Sun & BH Mon 10–5.30; Nov–Dec, 10–4. Weather permitting

www.nationaltrust.org.uk

Given my time again, I would study architecture, such is my enjoyment of classical buildings – of which Stowe is blessed with more than its fair share! The magnificent early 18th-century grounds were created by some of the top landscapers and architects of the day, including John Vanbrugh, William Kent and Lancelot 'Capability' Brown. Many miles of well-fashioned lawns, lakes, woodlands and fields are embellished with temples, pavilions, monuments and bridges to create an idealized English scene. The Temple of Concord

and Victory, the Gothic Temple, the Palladian Bridge, the Rotondo and many more are glimpsed along carefully planned vistas as you journey through the parkland. This is England at its finest.

Battery-operated buggies are available for visitors with disabilities, but they must be booked in advance.

Waddesdon Manor

Waddesdon, Aylesbury, Buckinghamshire HP18 0JH Tel 01296 653211
March to mid-Dec, Wed–Sun & BH Mon 10–5

www.waddesdon.org.uk

The Rothschild family had accumulated vast wealth by the late 19th century, when Baron Ferdinand built this 45-room manor house. A beautifully maintained parterre filled with brightly coloured bedding plants graces the terrace, in true Victorian style. Magnificent urns and statues also enhance the gardens. Within the carefully landscaped parkland you'll find a large ornamental aviary

with brilliant formal beds to rival the plumage of the exotic birds within. There is a rose garden, many wonderful trees and some imposing stables. You may feel Waddesdon would look more at home in the Loire Valley – this may not be a fashionable style today, but Waddesdon is a glorious example of Victorian opulence at its very best.

The shops at Waddesdon are fantastic – there is an excellent gift shop and a wine shop selling produce from all the Rothschild vineyards.

The Savill Garden

The Great Park, Englefield Green, Windsor, Berkshire SL4 2HT Tel 01753 847518
Apr–Oct, daily 10–6; Nov–Mar daily 10–4 (closed 25–26 Dec)

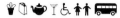

www.savillgarden.co.uk

In the 1930s Sir Eric Savill recognized the amazing potential of this undulating land for growing rhododendrons, azaleas, magnolias and a plethora of unusual and spectacular woodland plants, which are mainly at their best in April and May. Savill's successor, John Bond, continued to add features of interest, including the dry gravel garden, the fascinating collection of plants from New Zealand, the Silver Jubilee garden (planted with trees for autumn colour) and the Queen Elizabeth temperate house, stocked with non-hardy species. There are

alpine beds, alpine meadows, bog plantings, peat beds, mature trees, streams, lakes and much more. The herbaceous borders and the rose gardens are a blaze of colour during summer: this is truly a garden for all seasons.

The adjacent Valley Gardens are spectacular in azalea season, especially in the little dell known as the Punch Bowl.

Hatfield House

Hatfield, Hertfordshire, AL9 5NQ Tel 01707 287010
Easter Sat–Sep, daily 11–5.30. East Gardens Fri only

www.hatfield-house.co.uk

Hatfield House was built in 1611 by Robert Cecil, 1st Earl of Salisbury. We have reports of the magnificent gardens stocked with plants collected on the travels of Cecil's gardener, John Tradescant the Elder. Today, little remains of the earlier layout but

Mollie, Marchioness of Salisbury has spent decades recreating gardens sympathetic to the architecture and style of the Jacobean period. The West Gardens include the

complex box knots outside the Old Palace (built in the 1480s). Plants of that period surround a new central fountain. Statues in yew alcoves lead the way to pleached lime walks and

The Gardens of the Rose near St Albans hold a vast collection of roses, ancient and modern, miniature, shrub, climbing and

the hedged Privy Garden with its striking borders and central pool. The exquisite Scented Garden is filled with herbs, roses and lilies. The Wilderness – 3ha (7 acres) of meadow, bulbs, arboretum and shrubberies – makes a pleasant contrast to the formal gardens. It offers views of the south front, its gardens and the impressive avenue stretching into the distance through the park. This is, in brief, the sum of what you see when you visit on any day except Friday: lovely, but somehow incomplete. The East Gardens open only on Fridays, and comprise an organic kitchen garden with trained fruit trees, luscious citrus trees, vines and every other kind of quality produce. Double rows of lollipop evergreen oaks border the East Parterre, and box beds overflow with colourful roses and perennials. Beyond this lies the maze

(not open to the public), an orchard, the Mount Garden, and the New Pond (a lake to most of us!). Hatfield's gardens have the perfect blend of formal structure and sumptuous planting – a feast of fine horticulture.

everything in-between. The roses are beautiful, especially in June, but the gardens are a little unkempt (tel 01727 850461).

The Royal Botanic Gardens, Kew

The Royal Botanic Gardens, Kew, Richmond, Surrey TW9 3AB Tel 0208 332 5655

Daily from 9.30 (closed 24–25 Dec). Closing times vary

www.rbgkew.org.uk

A day at the world-famous and historic Royal Botanic Gardens is not long enough even to scratch the surface of this extraordinary and important institution, designated a UNESCO World Heritage Site in 2003.

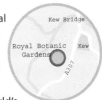

Kew is a living encyclopaedia of the world's flora, to be seen growing both in the gardens and in the array

of glasshouses, old and new. There are woodlands, lakes and ponds; a palace and a pagoda; and all manner of gardens in between, from the Lilac Garden, the Bamboo Garden and the Berberis Dell to the Winter Garden.

The glasshouses shelter an amazing collection of non-hardy plants. The Palm House, a remarkable Victorian structure

Parking is usually available in Kew Green/Brentford gate or in nearby residential areas. Nearest tube is Kew Gardens (District Line).

is filled with plants from the tropics. It also houses a collection of marine plantlife. The Alpine House is another favourite of mine, with a constantly changing display of flowering plants. The Princess of  Wales Conservatory is a state-of-the-art glasshouse containing 10 climatic zones, allowing plants from many diverse habitats to be grown. Here you pass from arid deserts to the steaming rain forest and see cacti and orchids, bananas and pineapples, aloes and agaves. The Temperate House, another Victorian masterpiece, has subtropical plants from the Antipodes, South America and South Africa. In summer the collection of ornamental aquatic plants in the Waterlily House includes some beautifully serene water lilies. In these very urban surroundings the gardens are a haven for wildlife. There are even badgers living at Kew. And how many other bluebell woods are there so close to the centre of a busy capital city?

Research, education, propagation, preservation, publication, conservation and more are all being carried out behind the scenes.

Hampton Court Palace

East Molesey, Surrey KT8 9AU Tel 0870 753 7777

Daily, dawn–dusk

www.hrp.org.uk

It is hardly necessary to introduce you to this extraordinary and significant royal palace. Do allow time to absorb the glories of its interior before venturing out to the gardens that surround this unique piece of British history. Initially, it is the immense scale of the borders, rose garden, fountains and canal that leaves you breathless. But nothing can steel you for the stunning formality of the parterres and yew spires of William III's Privy Garden. And take a look at the pergola – timberwork on a truly grand scale. My favourite areas are the pond gardens:

topiary, lime screens, knots, bedding plants and statues. This must surely have been where kings and queens sought romance, intimacy and refuge from their burdened lives.

The Hampton Court Flower Show in July is fantastic, but traffic and travel are awful! Visit the Palace Gardens at another time.

Painshill Park

Portsmouth Road, Cobham, Surrey KT11 1JE Tel 01932 868113
Mar–Oct, Tue–Sun & BH 10.30–6; Nov–Feb, Wed–Sun 11–4 (closed 25 Dec)

www.painshill.co.uk

I visited these gardens on a silent, misty March morning. I had the run of the place and could easily have been transported back to the 18th century as ruins and follies loomed above the lakes. Deer, squirrels, birds and waterfowl went carelessly about their business and the fingers of twisted ancient oaks and chestnuts reached out towards the watery sun.

This magical landscape is worth visiting at all times of year. It is not a plantsman's garden but a place to find peace, to

enjoy a picnic, to feed the swans, and to admire the vision of its creator, The Hon Charles Hamilton, who transformed this part of the Mole Valley into an Arcadian jewel.

got blisters because the walk is long and I wore the wrong shoes. wished I'd brought binoculars and some bread to feed the ducks.

The Royal Horticultural Society's Garden, Wisley

Woking, Surrey GU23 6QB Tel 01483 224234
Mar–Oct, daily 10–6 (Sat–Sun & BH 9–6); Nov–Feb 10–4.30 (closed 25 Dec)

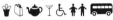

www.rhs.org.uk

The Royal Horticultural Society moved from London to its newly acquired country estate in Wisley at the turn of the 20th century. Since then the Society has enlarged and developed the land into a series of diverse and fascinating gardens, always maintained to the highest of standards. You can find at Wisley anything from borders and beds to rockeries and wild gardens; lakes and streams to orchards and arboreta. There are hills and valleys, vegetables and roses, model gardens

and glasshouses accommodating plants from all over the world. Notable recent additions are the borders created by Dutch designer Piet Oudolf, who is well known for

The Wisley collection of fruit cultivars now exceeds 1,300. The model fruit garden explains all you need to know to obtain the best

his prairie-style planting in large, natural drifts of colour. These borders are at their best in late summer. The Trials Field is always worth a visit. The varieties being put through their paces change over  time, and the neat rows of plants always look impressive when viewed from Battleston Hill. This is the place where the cream of Britain's horticultural experts assess plants for the prestigious 'Award of Garden Merit' (AGM) – the ultimate recognition of a plant's good character and garden worthiness. In the background at Wisley there are teams of dedicated scientists researching garden pests and diseases. Botanists supervise the Wisley Herbarium, a collection of preserved plants of great botanical importance. Eighty or more staff are employed in the grounds, assisted by 30 horticultural students and 100 volunteers.

Wisley is at the hub of the world of British horticulture and is a delight and an education to visit at any time of year. A large nursery sells a wide variety of high-quality plants.

yields from a small plot of land. Trees are trained in many space-saving ways, and container-grown fruits are displayed.

Hever Castle

Hever, near Edenbridge, Kent TN8 7NG Tel 01732 865224

Mar–Nov, daily 11–6 (Mar & Nov 11–4). Last entry 1 hour before close

www.hevercastle.co.uk

I adore the gardens at Hever – the former home of Anne Boleyn and, 400 years later, of William Waldorf Astor. This perfect moated castle, dating back to the 13th century, looks more Hollywood than Garden of England! Astor bought the Hever estate in 1903 and spent a sizeable chunk of his immense wealth on turning it into the impressive sight we see today. He tacked on the 'Tudor' village and in the early years of the 20th century created the spectacular Italian-style gardens as a forum for his collection of classical statues. One thousand

men worked to implement the design by Joseph Cheal and Son.

Adjacent to the exasperating maze and the topiary by the castle there are a number of hedged, intimate

The Pompeiian Wall houses many ancient pieces of sculpture and architectural antiquities. It is one eighth of a mile long. The

gardens laid out as they might have been in Tudor times. The Rhododendron Walk and Spring Garden lead away from the castle and up the hill, accommodating magnificent trees, many of which are now reaching huge proportions. The tranquil half-moon pond hides the truly remarkable gardens beyond. Here we discover the Pompeiian Wall. With its ruined follies, ancient statues set in enclosures and stunning planting, it runs alongside a vast lawn decorated with formal ponds and more statuary. A long pergola stretches down the other side of the lawn, shaded by beautifully trained vines and roses. From here you can enter the rose garden, which is breathtakingly lovely and filled with scent from a plethora of varieties. The Italianate loggia is heaven on earth – a piazza whose steps curve round a fountain embellished with nymphs, and whose pillared colonnades stretch across the end of the 14ha (35-acre) lake. There are many other fine borders and romantic spaces, as well as a water maze in which children can get thoroughly and happily soaked!

Long Border has been planted in Edwardian style in a rainbow of colours and provides year-round attraction.

Penshurst Place Gardens

Penshurst, Tonbridge, Kent TN11 8DG Tel 01892 870307
Apr–Nov, daily 10.30–6; Mar, Sat–Sun 10.30–6

www.penshurstplace.com

Penshurst Place has been in the hands of the Sidney family for 450 years. The fine and ancient house is worth taking time to visit: the Barons' Hall, built in 1341, is considered to be the most complete example of 14th-century domestic architecture in England. Records show that a garden existed on this site as early as 1346, and much of the structure and layout of the present garden remains as it was in the 16th century.

The box-edged parterre beds in the splendid Italian garden complement the house, as does the central lily pond. It is oval in shape in order to appear a perfect circle when viewed from the house. From here, you pass through a series of yew-hedged rooms that shelter assorted schemes and planting, each with a distinctive style and character. A pair of herbaceous borders forms a colourful axis from which you can visit the rose garden and the Lanning Roper border (created by the American 20th-century garden designer). You then move on to the spring and autumn gardens, the particularly pretty Grey Garden, and 'Diana's Bath', a Victorian re-vamp of a former stewpond. Do not miss the stunning peony border when it is in season in early summer – what a show! Pass through the charming orchard that was so important historically at Penshurst, where apricots, peaches, plums, pears and apples were all grown as early as the 17th century.

Then view the Union Jack parterre, one of the most recent grand designs (best seen in spring and summer). Penshurst oozes history and atmosphere from every pore. The place is lovingly maintained and is a real pleasure to visit.

200 acres) in which to enjoy a family day out. There are many entertainments for the children and fine gardens for all to see.

Sissinghurst Castle Garden

Sissinghurst, Cranbrook, Kent TN17 2AB Tel 01580 710700

Mid-Mar to Oct, Mon–Tue & Fri 11–6.30, Sat–Sun & BH 10–6.30 (last entry 5.30 or dusk)

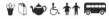

www.nationaltrust.org.uk

There can be few such famous gardens as Sissinghurst, home to poet and novelist Vita Sackville-West and her husband Harold Nicolson – diplomat, historian and diarist. The Elizabethan tower house and 160ha (400-acre) estate were in a state of near total decay when the Nicolsons first visited Sissinghurst

in 1930. Vita fell in love with the place and they purchased it three weeks later. As they restored the estate, Harold utilized the arches, walls and buildings to create a network of enclosures and vistas in a geometric and classical style. He also planted hedges and allées. It was Vita who set about furnishing the resulting spaces

There is a timed ticket system operational at peak times and you can expect a short wait. If possible, visit off-peak. There is limited

with soft and romantic planting in a loose informal style – a perfect foil to the hard lines created by her husband. Vita selected a colour scheme for each area: intense, scorching colours in the cottage garden, and pink, plum and lilac hues in the rose garden, with its blousy romance and heady scents. It is the White Garden that is most famous:

it is elegant and yet dramatic, safe and intimate but also, in its day, dangerously new and innovative. You'll find other areas of great peace, such as the mirror-calm moat pond and the verdant orchard planted with narcissi and wild flowers. There are mysterious passages of yew and tantalizing glimpses through clairvoie spaces in hedges and walls

The hugely influential gardens at Sissinghurst were the passion of two people who formed the perfect design partnership, creating what many believe is a near perfect garden.

access for wheelchairs (only two at a time) and no pushchairs are allowed. There are picnic areas near the car park.

Great Dixter

Northiam, Rye, East Sussex TN31 6PH Tel 01797 252878
Apr to mid-Oct, Tue–Sun 2–5.30, BH Sun–Mon 11–5.30

www.greatdixter.co.uk

The earliest surviving part of the house at Great Dixter dates from the 15th century, but it was in 1910 that Nathaniel Lloyd commissioned Edwin Lutyens to restore and extend the house and design the gardens. Derelict sheds and barns were transformed into attractive garden buildings, York stone paving and steps

were laid down, and yew hedges and topiary shapes were created (all of which are still visible). Today Great Dixter is home to the gardener, writer, and much-respected horticultural guru Christopher Lloyd.

Dixter reveals Lloyd's unmistakable passion for arranging plants of all kinds in inventive colour combinations. The paths and hedges, it seems, only just contain the unbridled and

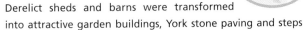

Note the very charming dachshunds formed in cobbles within the paving of the walled garden. And be sure to visit the nursery.

riotous mixed planting. In fact, of course, the borders are carefully controlled. They combine textures, foliage shapes and an assortment of colours, provided by shrubs, trees, grasses, perennials, bulbs and climbers. Head Gardener Fergus Garrett and his team expertly maintain vibrant colours throughout the season by using annuals and bedding plants to plug the gaps. This also means that the garden will never look the same on any two visits. The wildflower meadows are carpeted with native orchids (four species live here), and the Horse Pond has floating mats of water lilies. The Exotic Garden lives up to its name, planted with cannas, bananas, yuccas and dahlias, all in hot reds and oranges (these are best seen in late summer to autumn).

This is a marvellous garden, bursting with stimulating ideas, unfettered original colour schemes, intriguing and inspiring plants, and a huge sense of style. Dixter is the creation of a horticultural maverick and a great character.

During World War I Great Dixter became a hospital, and in World War II child evacuees used the Great Hall as a dormitory.

Leonardslee Lakes and Gardens

Lower Beeding, Horsham, West Sussex RH13 6PP Tel 01403 891212
Apr–Oct, daily 9.30–6 (last entry 4.30)

www.leonardslee.com

Leonardslee is the home of the Loder family and is synonymous with rhododendrons. Visit at peak flowering time (May) for a memorable experience. The steep-sided valley has a network of paths under a high canopy of trees that give the dappled shade preferred by rhododendrons. All shapes, sizes and colours of bloom are here, from bluest mauve to imperial purple, cerise to shell pink, brilliant crimsons, oranges and yellows – and big white trumpets with purple-spotted throats. It is a spectacular sight, and the

perfume is intoxicating. The rock garden is planted with evergreen Japanese azaleas, which flower so enthusiastically that their leaves disappear under cloaks of vibrant colour. Take your sunglasses!

The 'Loderi' group of rhododendrons, raised by Sir Edmund Lode in 1901, are considered to be particularly fine hybrids.

West Dean Gardens

Chichester, West Sussex PO18 0QZ Tel 01243 818210
May–Sep, daily 10.30–5; Mar–Apr & Oct 11–5 (last entry 4.30)

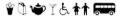

www.westdean.org.uk

Set in the rolling South Downs, this Edwardian house is run as a residential college. The gardens include vast lawns, mature trees, a pretty sunken garden and a spring garden. The 90m (300ft) pergola, designed by Harold Peto, is dressed in honeysuckle, clematis and roses. Add to this 97ha (240 acres) of parkland, woodland walks, an arboretum and an excellent visitor centre and you might be impressed. But it is the walled kitchen gardens that are the jewel in the crown. Beautifully restored Victorian glasshouses are filled with exotic plants, tender vegetables and fruit trees. Outside are

Singleton

A286

West Dean Gardens

▼ *Chichester*

neat rows of salad leaves, vegetables, flowers for cutting and fruit bushes. There are also glorious orchards and herbaceous borders. Everyone will enjoy a visit to West Dean Gardens.

West Dean runs many events including a garden fair and a Chilli Fiesta. Open-air theatre on summer evenings is also a popular attraction.

Nymans

Handcross, Haywards Heath, West Sussex RH17 6EB Tel 01444 400321
Mar–Oct, Wed–Sun & BH 11–6; Nov–Feb, Sat–Sun 11–4 (weather permitting)

www.nationaltrust.org.uk

The acclaimed gardens at Nymans were created in the first half of the 20th century. In 1947 the house, home to the Messel family, was largely destroyed by fire. One wing was subsequently restored and is now open to the public. The garden passed to the National Trust in 1953 after Leonard Messel's death.

Further disaster struck at Nymans in October 1987, when

the Great Storm destroyed hundreds of trees and much of the garden. But with hindsight one sees that the storm actually gave Nymans a new lease of life – it let more light in and made more water available for the surviving planting. Most importantly, it provided opportunities for change. Today the gardens are absolutely stunning.

Many plants have been named after Nymans and its people
Eucryphia x *nymansensis* 'Nymansay', *Magnolia* x *loebneri* 'Leonar

A pinetum has been planted to replace the previous one, along with many more rare and interesting trees. Miraculously, the lime avenue survived, and from a viewing platform at one end you get spectacular views over the Sussex countryside and the Nymans bluebell woods (which are a great spectacle in May). The famous pergola was inspired by the Japanese Exhibition of 1903, and drips with roses and wisteria. It adjoins the croquet lawn that is surrounded by rhododendrons, pieris and heather borders. The Wall Garden, with its Italianate fountain flanked by topiary yews, is the oldest part of the garden. It is wildly colourful in summer, when the borders are at their best. An assortment of rare and wonderful trees and shrubs thrive within the walls, including a collection of South American plants. The rose garden, renovated after being badly damaged by fallen trees in the storm, is filled with scented old-fashioned varieties and is embellished with complementary perennials and a pretty central fountain.

My favourite parts of the gardens at Nymans are the intimate, scented walled forecourt and the beautiful box knot gardens, which are enclosed by a crenellated yew hedge. The ruins of the house are tragically romantic and are swathed with climbers scrambling through empty window frames.

Messel' and *Camellia* 'Leonard Messel' all hold the Award of Garden Merit given by the RHS to 'plants of outstanding garden value'.

Exbury Gardens

Exbury, Southampton SO45 1AZ Tel 02380 891203/899422 (information line)

Mar to mid-Nov, daily 10–5.30 (or dusk); mid-Nov to Dec, Sat–Sun 10–4

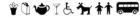

www.exbury.co.uk

Still in the hands of the de Rothschild family, Exbury was established by Lionel de Rothschild between the wars. Some 80ha (200 acres) of woodland gardens are planted predominantly with the rhododendrons and azaleas for which the gardens (and Rothschilds) are justifiably famous. They are simply spectacular during May. The brightly coloured plantings around lakes and ponds and in the woodland glades are a delight for all. There are also some very fine trees and many more plant varieties to see. An autumn visit is highly recommended to admire the wonderful

leaf colours of the Japanese maples and to see the nerine collection, which flowers in October. Prairie-style borders are a new addition, and are at their best from mid- to late summer.

The delightful Apple Court Nursery near Lymington (tel 0159 642130) specializes in grasses, hostas and hemerocallis.

The Manor House

Upton Grey, Hampshire RG25 2RD Tel 01256 862827

Apr–Oct, Mon–Fri by appointment only

http://website.lineone.net/~uptongrey-garden

In 1908, aged 65 and at the peak of her career, Gertrude Jekyll, one of Britain's most influential designers, was commissioned to design these gardens. Meticulously restored to the original plans (on display), they are now perhaps the finest example of her work.

North of the house lies the wild garden, where mown paths meander through long grass and wild flowers, with rambler

roses tumbling over timber supports. The formal gardens are terraced with drystone walls and bounded by yew hedges. Soft pink peonies, lilies and roses in square beds are framed by woolly-leaved stachys. Along the sides, herbaceous borders are planted in Jekyll's drifts of merging colours. The plants are all of the period and well

Celebrated garden designer Gertrude Jekyll (1843–1932) wrote about "the enduring happiness that the love of a garden gives".

Mottisfont Abbey Garden

Mottisfont, Romsey, Hampshire SO51 0LP Tel 01794 340757
Jun, daily 11–8.30; Mar–May, Sat–Wed 11–6; Jul–Aug, Sat–Thu 11–6; Sep–Oct, Sat–Wed 11–dusk

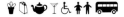

www.nationaltrust.org.uk

Mottisfont Abbey is famous as the home of old-fashioned roses, and during the mid-summer months the old walled kitchen garden is awash with scent and colour as hundreds of roses burst into bloom. Portland, damask, china, moss, gallicas, albas, ramblers, climbers and so many more fill the borders and shroud the walls. There are drifts of scented pinks and salvias, and good herbaceous planting to complement the roses. Box hedges, yew pillars and gravel paths add structure.

Beyond the walls, the fine old abbey stands in rolling lawns

by a tributary of the River Test. The lawns boast some gigantic trees, particularly the London plane whose girth is about 12m (40ft) and whose branches cast shade over a third of an acre.

Longstock Park Water Gardens, near Stockbridge (tel 01264 810894) are open only two Sundays per month but are well worth visiting.

Sir Harold Hillier Gardens

Jermyns Lane, Ampfield, Romsey, Hampshire SO51 0QA Tel 01794 368787

Daily 10.30–6,(or dusk). Closed 25–26 Dec

www.hillier.hants.gov.uk

This vast collection of trees and shrubs, some of which are very rare and unusual, covers some 70ha (180 acres). It is the remarkable legacy of the late Sir Harold Hillier, who in the 1950s started a nursery in what was then a 1ha (2-acre) garden. The winter garden is inspirational, and the boggy valley leading to the lake is wonderful in spring and summer. Magnolias, camellias and rhododendrons bloom from winter to early summer. There are maples, pines, witch hazels, flowering dogwoods and daphnes,

as well as broad herbaceous borders, and scree and heather beds, clearly labelled and well maintained. This is a lovely place to wander in, and it continues developing and improving.

The Gurkha Memorial Garden has Nepalese planting, and a traditional Chautara (resting place) displaying regimental badges.

West Green House Garden

West Green, Hartley Wintney, Hook, Hampshire RG27 8JB Tel 01252 844611
Apr–Aug, Thu–Sun & BH Mon 11–4.30; Sep 1–4.30

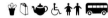

www.nationaltrust.org.uk

Within the walled garden of this delightful English manor house is a vibrant tapestry of annuals and perennials in formal borders. Colour is Marylyn Abbott's forte, and the range of hues from deepest plum, violet and blue, to yellow, cream and white is truly breathtaking. The potager brims with salads, vegetables and flamboyant flowers surrounding the ornamental fruit cages.

An *Alice in Wonderland* garden has red-and- white planting and topiary characters. This garden, like Marylyn, has a huge sense of fun. In contrast, the grounds surrounding the walled garden are calm and serene. The formal ponds and rills of the Nymphaeum and the lakes and shady walks beyond offer quiet and cool places to stroll.

Visit the charming cottage garden (at the end of the car park created by West Green gardener Dave Chase.

Heale House

Middle Woodford, near Salisbury, Wiltshire SP4 6NT Tel 01722 782504
Tue–Sun & BH Mon 10–5

www.gardens-guide.com

The River Avon meanders through the gardens of Heale House, the 16th-century home of the Rasch family. The beautiful 3ha (8-acre) grounds include the Tunnel Garden, an attractive walled kitchen garden so named because of the apple and pear tree tunnels. The water gardens contain many interesting bulbs and trees, and a large Japanese tea-house surrounded by magnolias and moisture-loving plants straddles a channel of the Avon. The terraces and gardens around the house are

laid out in a formal style with balustrades and York stone paving, but the whole is softened by burgeoning borders and self-sown plants that grow wherever they fall. Roses ramble happily everywhere.

Visit the Heale House plant centre, which is a horticultural Aladdin's cave of quality plants, including the unique 'Terrace' roses.

Iford Manor

Bradford-on-Avon, Wiltshire BA15 2BA Tel 01225 863146
May–Sep, Tue–Thu, Sat–Sun & BH 2–5; Apr & Oct, Sun 2–5

www.ifordmanor.co.uk

The Arts and Crafts architect Harold Peto (1854–1933) believed that a garden should be a combination of architecture and plants. After training as an architect, he worked in partnership with Ernest George (employing Edwin Lutyens as an assistant), before turning to garden design in the 1890s. Peto was a great collector, making fequent visits to Italy, and in 1899 he found a home for his classical statuary and architectural fragments in Iford Manor, a small Palladian-style house on the River Frome at

the foot of a steep tree-covered slope. The Edwardian era was a period of great enthusiasm for Italian gardens, and Peto was heavily influenced by Classical and Renaissance styles. He transformed

Walk a little way into the woods just above the garden to seek out the restored Japanese garden. Enjoy the contrast between

the hillside at Iford Manor into a series of nostalgic terraces, incorporating steps, rills, loggias, pools, urns and statues. He also built the cloisters, a place of enormous peace and serenity, in the 13th-century Romanesque style. But overall, Peto never lost touch with the fact that Iford Manor is essentially English. He has, quite simply, created English gardens with a strong Italian accent. The result is breathtaking.

Planting is often architectural but it incorporates exclamation marks of colour in every season, and surprises are revealed around every corner. The statues, pots and stonework are varied and interesting: some are ancient and some are fine copies of great, familiar classics commissioned by Harold Peto for Iford. Iford Manor gardens are an extraordinary example of an

Edwardian scheme in the Italianate style. Peto has created a beautiful, elegant and historic jewel in the crown of British garden design, and the current owners do an excellent job of maintaining this.

the formality of Peto's creation and the rural views it offers over the meadows of the Frome valley, grazed by cattle.

Stourhead

Stourton, Warminster, Wiltshire BA12 6QF Tel 01747 841152

Daily 9–7 (or dusk)

www.nationaltrust.org.uk

The grounds were developed by Henry Hoare (of the banking family) in the mid-18th century and there are few such fine examples of the English landscape garden.

I cannot keep away from Stourhead. That first uplifting glimpse of the Arcadian landscape is irresistible: the Palladian stone bridge reflected in the lake and the majestic Pantheon beyond. As you follow the footpath along the wooded valley you encounter new, exciting vistas at every turn: a rustic cottage, a temple, a grotto. You pass an

array of plants from all over the world, including conifers of vast proportions, azaleas, rhododendrons and other rare trees and shrubs that thrive in this sheltered place.

The wide lawns leading down to the lake make a lovely place for a picnic. Don't forget to bring some bread for the ducks.

Abbotsbury Sub-Tropical Gardens

Abbotsbury, Weymouth, Dorset DT3 4LA Tel 01305 871387

Mar–Oct, daily 10–6; Nov–Feb 10–4 (last entry 1 hour before close). Closed 25–26 Dec & 1 Jan

www.abbotsbury-tourism.co.uk

As you approach Abbotsbury you pass along coastal roads where trees have been blown into wizened shapes and hedges are stunted and salt-burned. The gardens are a totally unexpected oasis. Shelterbelts of trees have made this valley, so close to the sea, a haven for tender species. There are many thousands of remarkable plants to admire in this collection, built up over several centuries. Magnolias are the size of oaks, and tree ferns and palms jostle for space between bamboos and bananas. Streams, bogs and ponds also add much interest. Golden

pheasants strut around, and the distant call of a kookaburra (in the aviary by the tea room) adds an exotic touch. The gardens are well signed and labelled.

Mapperton (tel 01308 862645), 5 miles northeast of Bridport, is worth visiting. The terraced valley with pools and topiary is unique.

Athelhampton House

Athelhampton, Puddletown, Dorchester DT2 7LG Tel 01305 848363
Mar–Oct, Mon–Thu 10–5, Fri 10–3.30, Sun 10.30–5, BH 10–5.30; Nov–Feb, Sun 10.30–dusk

www.athelhampton.co.uk

The gardens around this Tudor manor house are bounded on three sides by the River Piddle, and water certainly features strongly here, with ponds and a canal to enjoy. Elizabethan in appearance, the gardens were actually designed by Francis Inigo Thomas in 1891. Yew hedges, pleached limes and remarkable stone walls create the structure of the formal rooms, each a surprise and quite different from the last. Imaginative planting enhances and softens the lines, and there are some unusual and tender species to be seen. The giant yew pyramids in the

Great Court are well worth a visit. This place has a notable feeling of intimacy and history. The gardens are superbly maintained and the house is also open.

It goes without saying that all rivers and ponds are dangerous, especially to small children, who should be supervised at all times.

Cranborne Manor

Cranborne, Wimborne Minster, Dorset BH21 5PP Tel 01725 517248
Mar–Sep, Wed 9–5

www.cranborne.co.uk

John Tradescant the Elder was thought to have been involved in the early designs of Robert Cecil's garden, which still form the backbone to the layout of this delightful and historic place. The formality of pleached limes, pergolas, allées, hedges, knots and topiary is softened with luscious planting. There are sumptuous herbaceous borders, lavender, scented pinks, roses and clematis. Windows in the yew hedge along the Chalk Walk allow you glimpses of the meadows beyond the grounds,

and the mount in the Sundial Garden gives you splendid views of the surrounding downland. The Green Garden is cool, with miniature box hedges in an intricate knot, and the herb garden emits spicy bouquets.

John Tradescant the Elder visited northern Europe, the Mediterranean and Russia on plant collecting forays in the 17th century.

Forde Abbey

Chard, Somerset TA20 4LU Tel 01460 220231
Daily 10–4

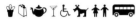

www.fordeabbey.co.uk

Sometimes you just know a garden is going to be exciting. As I approached the imposing 12th-century Cistercian abbey with its rambling Gothic additions, nothing could have prepared me for the sight that I beheld. Great swathes of mauve crocus cover the lawns – they are everywhere, in their millions. A blanket of *Cyclamen coum* shrouds the large rockery, their ears back as though unimpressed by the performance of their bulbous neighbours.

This is an early-spring spectacle not to be missed. I made a resolution to return to Forde Abbey in the summer as well, in order to appreciate fully the arboretum, the large borders, the alpine plants in

During the dissolution of the monasteries in the 16th century, Forde Abbey and its land were seized by Henry VIII. The Crown then

the rock garden, and the glories of the lakes and bog gardens. The spectacular formal Long Pond is flanked by Irish yew 'soldiers' and double borders planted with blooms of red, scarlet, orange and yellow in an explosion of colour. The magnum opus is the unparalleled view from the Ionic temple down the Long Pond and over the abbey beyond. There are extensive kitchen gardens (whose generous produce supplies the restaurant and house) and a good nursery selling unusual and tender plants. The abbey itself (open for some of the year) was transformed at the time of the Commonwealth into a magnificent country house groaning with exquisite pictures, the finest furniture and large important tapestries.

And yet Forde is very much a family home, as it has been for over three centuries. It oozes atmosphere and history, and I recommend a visit at any time of year. You will be made very welcome.

Greencombe

Porlock, Somerset TA24 8NU Tel 01643 862363
Apr–Jul & Oct–Nov, Sat–Wed 2–6 (also by appointment)

www.porlock.co.uk/greencombe

Some gardens are beautiful. Others are filled with great rarities. One or two are special because the owner is charismatic, a mine of information and ready to enjoy a chat and point out plants of seasonal interest.

Greencombe has all these qualities, and more. On a north-facing hill overlooking the Bristol Channel, these gardens were created largely by Joan Loraine. Some plants have been discovered so recently that they have no name, but every plant grows to double the size that it does anywhere else:

clematis blooms are the size of soup plates, and roses have reached the tops of the tallest trees. A giant leptospermum glows pink amongst the plethora of rare shrubs and plants. Take time to chat to Joan: she is utterly delightful and very knowledgeable.

There are so many unusual plants to remember that you'll need to bring a pencil with you, or that essential garden tool, a video camera.

Hadspen Garden and Nursery

Castle Cary, Somerset BA7 7NG Tel 01749 813707

Mar–Sep, Thu–Sun & BH Mon 10–5

www.hadspengarden.freeserve.co.uk

This remarkable garden has been developed and expanded since 1987 by Canadians Nori and Sandra Pope. They are best known for colour, and they use it to full effect throughout the year, creating opulent drifts of choice plantings. The borders have blocks of single colour, each shade merging into the next, from deepest plum to silver and white. Hadspen has been described as the greatest colour garden since Sissinghurst.

But there is more on offer than simply colour. There are varied textures and patterns, bog plants, a lily pond and a wildflower meadow. The garden is groaning

with desirable plants, some of which originated at Hadspen, and the nursery offers a good selection. The tulip season is a great time to visit.

Colour by Design, **Nori and Sandra's book on colour in the garden, is filled with inspirational planting ideas and colour schemes.**

Tintinhull Garden

Farm Street, Tintinhull, Yeovil, Somerset BA22 9PZ Tel 01935 822545
Apr–Sep, Wed–Sun & BH Mon 12–6

www.nationaltrust.org.uk

This elegant 18th-century house is built of sunshine-coloured local stone and stands in under 1ha (2 acres) of garden designed by Phyllis Reiss in the 1930s in the 'Hidcote' style. More recently, gardening guru Penelope Hobhouse lived at Tintinhull.

A number of hedged and walled rooms are linked by a grid of paths, which lead to eye-catching features – pretty seats and stone pavilions. Planting within each enclosure is brilliantly colour co-ordinated. Luxuriant perennials in the Eagle Court are enhanced by acid green euphorbias and box domes. There is a gold garden, white borders and a pool flanked by plantings in vibrant reds and yellow or soft blue and mauve, all linked by silver foliage. Throughout, there are interesting plant associations. Look out for the delightful kitchen garden and cider orchard. There's plenty to admire in such a small acreage.

Penelope Hobhouse now lives in Dorset. She is a gardener, designer highly commended writer, international lecturer and historian.

Coleton Fishacre

Brownstone Road, Kingswear, Dartmouth TQ6 0EQ Tel 01803 752466
Apr–Oct, Wed–Sun & BH Mon 10.30–5.30; Mar, Sat–Sun 11–5

www.nationaltrust.org.uk

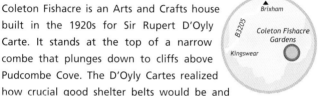

Coleton Fishacre is an Arts and Crafts house built in the 1920s for Sir Rupert D'Oyly Carte. It stands at the top of a narrow combe that plunges down to cliffs above Pudcombe Cove. The D'Oyly Cartes realized how crucial good shelter belts would be and established them even before the house was completed. Formal terraces and walls are planted with myrtles, michelias and camellias, and from the rill garden a stream tumbles down the valley between iris, gunnera and Himalayan cowslips. Trees

clothe the valley sides, the ground carpeted with bluebells and three-cornered leeks. This is not for the fainthearted – down to the cliffs and back was enough for me, but paths criss-cross the garden too.

The award-winning, family-run orchid growers Burnham Nurseries Ltd are based near Newton Abbott (tel 01626 352233).

The Garden House

Buckland, Monachorum, Yelverton, Devon PL20 7LQ Tel 01822 854769
Mar–Oct, daily 10.30–5 (last entry 4.30)

www.thegardenhouse.org.uk

Lionel and Katharine Fortescue started to create these gardens around the ruins of a 16th-century vicarage in 1946. Since the 1980s Keith Wiley and his wife Ros have developed them further. The walled garden houses a wide range of interesting plants, while architectural features include the much-photographed Ovals Garden and the vicarage ruins. Beyond the walls there is a South African garden, awash with blooms from the veldt;

the quarry garden; wild gardens, including the Devon lane; the Cretan Cottage Garden, and much more. Look for the Magic Circle, a space of serenity and calm. Keith veers towards the new style of perennial planting, and there can be few more pleasant places in which to experience successful and interesting plant combinations.

This garden is on the edge of Dartmoor and close to Plymouth. If you're on holiday in the West Country, make a detour.

Knightshayes

Bolham, Tiverton, Devon EX16 7RQ Tel 01884 254665
Mid-Mar to Oct, daily 11–5.30

www.nationaltrust.org.uk

Knightshayes
Court

A361

Tiverton

This late 19th-century house stands solidly in the Devon hills. Steep-banked terraces decorated with topiary and herbaceous borders give way to undulating parkland. Statues and urns enhance all the formal gardens, but perhaps the most famous feature is the topiary fox racing round the top of a hedge ahead

of a pack of hounds. The house is clad in interesting climbers, and yew hedges enclose the alpine border, pool and the paved gardens. The extensive woodland gardens comprise shade-loving perennials, bulbs, and interesting trees and shrubs. A conservatory to the east of the house is furnished with ferns and flowering plants from warmer climes. An excellent garden.

The house is a fine example of the Victorian gothic style, so be sure to allow time to look around inside too.

Marwood Hill Gardens

Barnstaple, North Devon EX31 4EB Tel 01271 342528
Daily, dawn–dusk (closed 25 Dec)

www.marwoodhillgarden.co.uk

This peaceful Devon valley is a plantsman's paradise. An interesting arboretum clothes the steep grassy banks, underplanted with spring bulbs and wild flowers. The stream in the valley floor trickles through a series of ponds and bogs crammed with a delicious array of moisture lovers, including the national collections of

Iris ensata and astilbe. Alpine scree beds, herbaceous borders and a wisteria-covered pergola add to the enjoyment, and the walled garden contains an excellent plant centre. This is a garden for everyone, not just the connoisseur – there are plenty of places to sit and enjoy the magnificent gardens and the country views.

The Royal Horticultural Society's garden at Rosemoor, near Grea Torrington, is very worthy of a visit (tel 01805 624067).

Cotehele Garden

St Dominick, Saltash, Cornwall PL12 6TA Tel 01579 351346
Daily 10.30–dusk

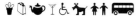

www.nationaltrust.org.uk

Cotehele stands at the head of a wooded valley sloping down to the River Tamar. Built between 1485 and 1627, the stone house, walls and domed dovecote provide an ancient and romantic setting for the gardens. In early spring the Daffodil Meadow lives up to its name, and daffodils are accompanied by crocus, snowdrops and cyclamen. Clouds of blossom cover the orchard, whose fruits are made into chutneys sold in the shop.

The Upper Garden, with its ornamental trees, herbaceous borders and lily pond comes into its own during summer. Sit on the terraces to enjoy the view over the valley garden, stewpond and woodland plantings of magnolias, camellias and rhododendrons.

Visit Cotehele Quay, to see an outstation of the National Maritime Museum, and Cotehele Mill to buy freshly ground organic flour.

Antony

Torpoint, Plymouth, Cornwall PL11 2QA Tel 01752 812191

Apr–Oct, Tue–Thu (also Jun–Aug, Sun) 1.30–5.30. Woodland Mar–Oct, Tue–Thu & Sat–Sun 11–5.30

www.nationaltrust.org.uk

Take the Torpoint car ferry from Plymouth and make this a day out to remember. Antony must be one of the most stunning houses situated in the most glorious position, both aesthetically, and also for the climatic benefits of the garden. Torpoint is a

finger of land surrounded by estuaries and the sea. Antony has fine views down broad avenues of trees, through the woodland garden and over the tidal River Lynher below.

As the land falls away to the water in a series of dingles and hollows, it is cloaked with maples, camellias, rhododendrons and all manner of trees and shrubs for the connoisseur. The waterfront is flanked by vast pines and evergreen oaks. Winding paths lead

You can also reach Antony by land from the west. Torpoint is very worthwhile exploring. Take the coastal road along the south side you past a Georgian Bath house and salt pans, and there are seats on which to take in the views and wonder at the incredible variety of interesting plants.

As you walk back up towards the house, the woodland gives way to wide parkland with enormous, old specimen trees. This ultimately meets the formal terraces to the north side of the house, where, in the shelter of the building, you'll find fine herbaceous borders and roses. On the top terrace there is a brave, contemporary water cone fountain by the brilliant William Pye that has perhaps rightly become Antony's most famous landmark. There is a superb knot garden and other hedged rooms to see as well as a Japanese garden and the Summer Garden, housing shrub roses and excellent 'country-house planting'.

The house is open and very well worth a visit. Antony sits majestically in this westerly corner of England, exuding a feeling of well-being, which is reflected in the courteousness of the staff and the smile on your face when you leave.

for clifftop views. Visit Mount Edgcumbe House and Country Park (tel 01752 822236) while you are in the area.

Heligan

'The Lost Gardens of Heligan', Pentewan, St Austell, Cornwall PL26 6EN Tel 01726 845100
Daily from 10 (closed 24–25 Dec). Closing times vary

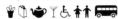

www.heligan.com

Thanks to Tim Smit and his team, Heligan is not 'lost' any more. The thrilling restoration of the 19th-century grounds was recorded live on television during the 1990s. This exciting, ambitious project continues today. The gardens are extensive: you'll need a day to

see them all. Explore the Jungle and Lost Valley to find exotic plants including palms, bamboos and massive tree ferns. The large kitchen gardens have greenhouses, coldframes, melon and peach houses, pineapple pits, bothies and potting

sheds filled with antique tools. There are ornamental gardens and a man-made rockery 90m (100yd) long. Heligan is a slice of horticultural history that has been brought back to life.

Visit Tim Smit's miraculous Eden Project near St Austell. Go at an off-peak time as it gets extremely crowded (tel 01726 811911).

Pine Lodge Gardens and Nursery

Holmbush, St Austell, Cornwall PL25 3RQ Tel 01726 73500
Mar–Oct, daily 10–6 (last entry 5)

www.pine-lodge.co.uk

Pine Lodge is a collection of gardens created since 1976 by Raymond and Shirley Clemo. The 12ha (30 acres) hold an impressive 6,000 varieties, all labelled clearly. There are formal pools and fountains; informal wildlife ponds; a bridge draped in white wisteria; a Japanese garden; an arboretum and pinetum; a large lake and

endless secret corners. Many tender plants can be found here, enjoying the warmth and shelter of St Austell Bay. Camellia, embothrium, dicksonia, leptospermum, abutilon, and large-leaved rhododendron thrive, among many other species. Scented plants are a speciality and there is fragance year-round. It is an extremely interesting garden to visit and the nursery is top-notch.

Leptospermums are evergreen shrubs, mainly from the Antipodes. They produce a profusion of tiny red, pink or white flowers.

Trebah Garden

Mawnan Smith, near Falmouth, Cornwall TR11 5JZ Tel 01326 250448

Daily 10.30–6.30 (last entry 5)

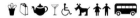

www.trebah-garden.co.uk

Trebah is one of the very best of Cornwall's gardens. Created in 1826 by Charles Fox, the estate thrived until its sale in 1939, when it was divided up. For some decades thereafter it changed hands regularly. This was a blessing in disguise, for it allowed the framework of the garden to mature uninterrupted, and is the reason why so many 'giants' are found here today. Luckily for us and our garden heritage, in 1981 Tony and Eira Hibbert acquired Trebah and set about its restoration.

Mawnan Smith
Falmouth ▲
Trebah Garden

After several years' devoted toil, the Hibberts opened the doors of this 11ha (26-acre) sub-tropical paradise to the public. They have safeguarded the future of the garden by forming a trust, and they continue to occupy the handsome, white

Tony Hibbert has named areas after Dutch friends, who helped him escape after being captured at Arnhem Bridge in World War II. You

94

house that stands at the top of the valley, with lovely views down to Polgwiddon Cove and the Helford estuary.

Banks of hydrangeas swathe the lawns below the house, and a network of paths leads you through the gardens. There are ponds and bog gardens, bamboo groves and a Gunnera Tunnel, where you walk under enormous specimens of these Brazilian 'dinosaur food' leaves that can measure 2.5m (8ft) across. You'll find tree ferns so mature that one even has a substantial rhododendron growing out of its stem! The rhododendrons are gargantuan – a grove where some reach up to 18m (60ft) makes quite a memorable sight.

All in all, this is a magical garden with wondrous old trees and shrubs to admire, places to sit and enjoy the views and much to keep the plant enthusiast happy. The facilities are excellent and there is a children's play area.

can still find slit trenches at Trebah, dug by the Americans in 1944 to protect their embarkation beach.

Trewithen

Grampound Road, Truro, TR2 4DD Tel 01726 883647

Mar–Sep, Mon–Sat 10–4.30 (also Apr–May, daily)

www.trewithengardens.co.uk

Included in this guidebook are a few gardens that are spectacular for a relatively short season. This is one such place: because while there is always something to see at Trewithen, like many woodland gardens it is at its peak between March and late June. This is the magical juncture when the vast camellias, magnolias, rhododendrons and azaleas are in full bloom, the new leaves of the trees are as soft as puppies' ears, and the pieris glow brilliant red among the unfurling fronds of ferns. Stewartia, leptospermum, embothrium, enkianthus and kalmia all jostle for space under the canopy of ornamental trees.

The 14ha (35-acre) collection compiled by George Johnstone in the early part of the last century includes specimens brought back principally from China and the Far East by famous plant-hunters such as George Forrest and Frank Kingdon-Ward. The

Caerhays Castle Garden, home of the famous *Camellia* x *williamsi* and some spectacular woodland planting is open Mar–May,

96

justly famous gardens at nearby Caerhays Castle were created by L C Williams, a close friend of Johnstone and a contributor to the gardens at Trewithen.

Unusually for a Cornish garden, the land is relatively flat, so viewing platforms have been constructed to allow you panoramas of the planting from above. The woodland gardens are surrounded by splendid parkland – a beautiful setting for the fine Georgian house. A comprehensive plant list is available and the labelling is good. The nursery offers a wide range of quality plants. There is also a private walled garden (used by the family but open occasionally during June and July) with roses and a herb garden.

Trewithen is definitely a garden for the enthusiast – it is privately owned, very well maintained and continues to be developed for future generations. A camera obscura will add an extra dimension for visitors in years to come.

daily 10–5.30. Check for details (tel 01872 501310 or visit www. caerhays.co.uk). The castle is also well worth a visit.

Tresco Abbey

Tresco, Isles of Scilly TR24 0QQ Tel 01720 424105

Daily 10–4

www.tresco.co.uk

Tresco Abbey Garden is a spectacular 7ha (17-acre) sub-tropical paradise with a world-famous collection of plants.

The island of Tresco is warmed by the Gulf Stream and enjoys a great deal of sunshine, very little frost, and some 760mm (30in) of rain per year. It is this unique and benign climate that enables a vast range of tender plants to be grown: there are over 20,000 exotic plants, and even at winter equinox more than 300 will be flowering. In spite of the disastrous losses incurred in

the freak cold weather of 1987 and during the gales of 1990 (when 800 trees came down), the gardens have bounced back and species from more than 80 countries around the world can be seen thriving here. Giant

Evidence of many local shipwrecks can be seen in the Valhalla ship's figurehead collection, located within the abbey gardens.

echiums, aloes, palms and a myriad of lush, exotic flowers jostle for space on the rocky banks and the terraced slopes. Trees from Chile, Australia and New Zealand tower overhead, forming shelter for bromeliads and tender camellias. Proteas, banksias and a teeming display of daisies from South Africa flower throughout the year. Giant bamboos and shrubs cloaked in vermilion blooms are the backdrop for bumper-sized pelargoniums, watsonias and crinums. The ruined abbey walls are swathed in climbers, and every fissure in the stonework is occupied by colourful succulents.

Tresco Abbey has been the home of the Dorrien-Smith family since the 1830s. They continue to enhance and develop this fascinating collection with empathy and skill. Do try to visit these gardens – marvellous at any time of year. You can fly by helicopter direct to Tresco from Penzance, or travel by ferry from Penzance to St Mary's Island and onwards by boat to Tresco.

Echium pininana is a biennial that grows blue flower spikes up to 3.5m (11ft) tall – hence its common name, Tower of Jewels.

"...try and learn a little from everybody and every place."

Northern England

Belsay Hall, Castle and Gardens

Belsay, Newcastle upon Tyne NE20 0DX Tel 01661 881 636

Apr–Sep, daily 10–6; Oct, daily 10–5; Nov–Mar, daily 10–4 (closed 24–25 Dec & 1 Jan)

www.english-heritage.org.uk

The early 19th-century Belsay Hall may not be the most breathtaking of houses, but its gardens are truly beautiful. Formal terraces around the hall are a charming contrast to the parkland and rhododendron gardens. A winter garden edges the peaceful croquet lawn, and through a door in a wall you find the magical Quarry Garden. Here, winding paths take you past towering rock faces, boulder arches, and unusual plantings that include magnolias, flowering

dogwoods, eucryphia, enkianthus, bamboos and even palm trees. Gunnera and other exotic bog plants thrive in ponds and streams, and climbers scramble up the cliff-like walls. Blinking and amazed, you emerge from the quarry into handsome Northumbrian countryside and take a path to the old castle – in itself magnificent.

Another quarry garden crammed with interesting plants has been created on a cottage-garden scale at Bide-a-Wee (tel 01670 772262).

Herterton House

Hartington, Cambo, Morpeth NE61 4BN Tel 01670 774278
May–Sep, Fri–Mon & Wed 1.30–5.30

www.gardens-guide.com

Herterton House

B6342

▼ A696

The Lawleys have transformed an old Northumbrian farmstead into a ravishing series of garden rooms. The first is a cloister garden planted with many beguiling varieties of medicinal herbs and dye-producing plants nestling in a strong, structural framework. At the front of the house, among gold topiary spheres, a winter

garden offers matchless views over the Northumbrian hills. The 'Fancy Garden' has a box parterre and gazebo. But best of all is the flower garden, packed with blends of perennials: unusual, very pretty and, it seems, tough enough to survive the cold winters. Rows of these rare perennials are planted out in the nursery – point out what you fancy and some will be dug up for you.

Visit Wallington Garden, south of Cambo (tel 01670 773600), where there is an exceptionally interesting and pretty walled garden.

Howick Hall

Alnwick, Northumberland NE66 3LB Tel 01665 577285

Apr–Oct, daily 1–6

www.gardens-guide.com

As Howick Hall lies only a mile from the coast, the mild climate, rare frosts and shelter provided by broad bands of woodland allow a splendid array of tender trees and shrubs to flourish here. Drimys, embothrium and many species of rhododendron, magnolia and azalea grow contentedly in the woodland garden, and in spring there are lovely displays of daffodils flowering in the parkland. The gardens are at their best during May and early

June, but come into their own again in the late summer with hydrangeas and eucryphias, followed by dramatic autumn colours from a vast range of ornamental trees.

The terraces and borders around the house are also stunning during the summer months. The most interesting area is the pond and bog

Nearby Alnwick was very busy when I visited off-peak, so try to avoid obviously popular days. Take your children to see inside the

garden: a broad range of unusual moisture-loving plants, many of which are collected from the wild, have been skilfully planted to create a patchwork of colour. Howick Hall,  with its great variety of rare and fascinating plants, is undoubtedly a connoisseur's paradise. You will not find shops and adventure playgrounds here, but you might spot the family ponies, who snort and snuffle in their stalls adjacent to the loos. This is a magical and non-commercial garden.

Not far away, Alnwick Castle offers quite a contrast. Within old walls, the Duchess of Northumberland perpetuates her courageous project to create a contemporary and innovative 'garden for the people' with grand planting, a grand cascade and a very grand budget (in excess of £30 million). What has been achieved to date (including the rose and ornamental gardens) is splendid. I look forward to seeing the finished article, which will include a grass labyrinth, the Serpent and Poison gardens, the spiral feature and a garden for the senses.

ancient castle, which was used as a backdrop to the *Harry Potter* movies. It is crammed with history and interest.

Holehird Gardens

Patterdale Road, Windermere, Cumbria LA23 1NP Tel 01539 446008

Daily, dawn–dusk

www.cragview.demon.co.uk

Amazingly these large grounds are maintained entirely by volunteers – members of the Lakeland Horticultural Society – who have restored the gardens of this Victorian mansion (currently a Leonard Cheshire Home). The gardens form an impressive backdrop to the remarkable achievements of the society at Holehird.

The walled garden has island beds with small, ornamental trees underplanted with interesting perennials, annuals and bulbs.

Around the edges are broad mixed borders planted to suit the different aspects of the site, and the walls are adorned with climbers. Beyond are alpine houses and scree beds. Alpines are an overlooked group of

Cumbria has a very high rainfall (typically 1200–1500mm/47–59in a year) with warm summers and mild winters – not unlike Cornwall

106

plants that are, given sharp drainage, often as tough as old boots and incredibly pretty, not to mention frequently scented. This is a very fine display and offers year-round interest.

The upper gardens are planted with heathers, conifers and ferns under towering monkey-puzzle trees, and the collection of rhododendrons is glorious in late spring. Blue Himalayan poppies flourish among shrubs from the Andes including *Desfontainia* and *Crinodendron*. There are marvellous streams and ponds with waterside plantings, and a most impressive border planted with hostas and day lilies is shaded by a pocket-handkerchief tree *(Davidia)*. The national collections of astilbe and hydrangea (formed to identify and conserve these species) ensures that there is plenty of late summer and autumn interest, when these plants are dazzling.

There can be few gardens that command such dramatic views of the Lake District. Holehird Tarn, below the gardens, is not maintained by the society, but you can walk there from the lower part of the gardens and soak up the peaceful atmosphere while watching the water birds.

These are ideal growing conditions for mountain plants such as those from the Himalayas and the Andes. Most require acid soil.

Dalemain Historic House and Gardens

The Estate Office, Dacre, Penrith CA11 0HB Tel 01768 486450

Apr to mid-Oct, Sun–Thu 10.30–5

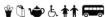

www.dalemain.com

The pink stone Georgian frontage hides a 12th-century pele tower built as a defence against marauding Scots. Landscaped parkland surrounds this beautiful family home. Along the southwest side is a deep ha-ha, topped by shrub roses and a stunning herbaceous border. A charming knot garden is tucked away by the children's garden, and the 250-year-old apple trees still bear fruit. The rose garden is heady with the scent of many old-fashioned varieties. If you happen to visit in early summer, look out for the blue Himalayan poppies massed among shrubs and ornamental trees. They are quite a sight. Some 10km (6 miles) north is Hutton-in-the-Forest (tel 01768 484449), a 17th-century hall built around a 13th-century pele tower. I recommend a visit to see the walled garden with its yew hedges, herbaceous borders, fruit trees and roses.

"...ponder on the past not as the past but as a pointer to the future." Geoffrey Jellicoe, leading landscape architect (1900–1996)

Levens Hall

Kendal, Cumbria LA8 0PD Tel 01539 60321
Apr to mid-Oct, Sun–Thu 10–5

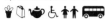

www.levenshall.co.uk

Levens Hall has been a family home for some 700 years. Both house and gardens brim with atmosphere and historical interest. Colonel James Grahme is reputed to have won the estate on the turn of a card, and he commissioned new formal gardens in 1688.

The topiary garden remains almost unchanged. Great yew mushrooms, chess pieces, lollipops, drums and cones loom out of box-edged spaces immaculately filled with vibrant

bedding plants. Beyond, there are herbaceous borders, age-old beech hedges, the Fountain Garden and more. The hedges and topiary take some five months to clip in the latter half of the year.

Look out for the ghosts (two ladies and a black woolly dog) that are frequently seen roaming around at Levens Hall.

Castle Howard

York YO60 7DA Tel 01653 648333

Daily, mid-Feb to Nov 10–4.30

www.castlehoward.co.uk

> Malton ▶
>
> Great Lake
>
> Castle Howard
>
> A64 ▼

At the start of the 18th century John Vanbrugh, a playwright, was commissioned by his friend, the 3rd Earl of Carlisle, to design his new country seat in the north of England. Castle Howard was, therefore, largely devised by a complete novice – not bad for a first attempt, for it is surely one of the finest houses in England.

The park and grounds can be divided into three parts. The first encompasses the temples, terraces, lakes and fountains within the pleasure grounds. A series of walks takes you from the staggeringly beautiful Atlas Fountain on

the south parterre (designed by W A Nesfield in the 1850s), past the south lake to Vanbrugh's Temple of the Four Winds (rather aptly named, as they can buffet you around in this bit

The house has extensive collections of pictures, furniture and porcelain. Castle Howard was featured in the famous 1980s

of Yorkshire, so dress up warm!). From here you have a fine view of the stunning New River Bridge and the even more impressive Mausoleum – designed by Hawksmoor – beyond.

The second area of great interest is Ray Wood. This was replanted by famous nurseryman James Russell in the mid-1970s with a huge and fascinating array of ericaceous shrubs and trees that come into their own during spring and early summer. The maze of winding pathways, echoing the irregular footpaths of the 18th-century wood, serves as a framework for the extensive, diverse collection of ornamental plantings.

The third area of note is the walled garden. It is now largely laid out as rose gardens: Lady Cecilia's Garden with its old-fashioned varieties, and the Sundial and Venus gardens, which are filled with 2,000 modern roses – all at their best during high summer. You are sure to be impressed by this magnificent house and splendid grounds. The children will enjoy the 'Myths and Monsters' tour of the many statues.

Newby Hall Gardens

Ripon, North Yorkshire HG4 5AE Tel 01423 322583
Apr–Sep, Tue–Sun & BH Mon 11–5.30 (also Jul–Aug, daily)

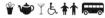

www.newbyhall.com

Newby's brochure boasts that its gardens are 'bordering on the sublime', and I certainly would not disagree. The handsome 17th-century house with its elegant Adam interior stands in landscaped park and rolling farmland, surrounded by what may be the best gardens north of the Watford Gap.

The Compton family and their ancestors have lived at Newby for more than 250 years, but it was Major Edward Compton

who, during the 1920s, set about creating much of the garden layout that we see today. Edward, his son Robin and his grandson Richard (the current occupant) have compiled an extraordinary

Two miles to the west of Ripon are Fountains Abbey and Studley Royal Water Gardens. The formal lakes and classical buildings form

collection of plants from all over the world and organized them into different areas. Stunning herbaceous borders make up the garden's central axis and drop down to the

River Ure. To either side can be found streams and water gardens, rockeries, walled gardens, rose gardens and pergolas, white gardens, tropical gardens, shrubberies and arboreta that blend seamlessly into each other to form a cohesive and enjoyable whole. At all times of year there are horticultural spectacles to enjoy at Newby, and the garden guidebook informs you of many plant names. The gardeners are also exceptionally knowledgeable and helpful.

It is easy for a tourist attraction to be spoilt by the obligatory visitor centre, restaurant, adventure playground and so forth. Newby has all these and even a mini railway, but they are top-quality and unobtrusive, and the staff are courteous and enthusiastic. Finally, there is an extremely good plant centre on the way out. You're sure to enjoy your visit.

a wonderful landscape that is embellished by the majestic ruins of the abbey and monastery at the head of the valley.

Parcevall Hall Gardens

Skyreholme, Skipton, North Yorkshire BD23 6DE Tel 01756 720311
Apr–Sep, daily 10–6; Oct, Sat–Sun 10–6. Last entry 5

www.parcevallhallgardens.co.uk

A garden should be looked at objectively, regardless of its surroundings. However, it would be churlish not to mention the journey to Parcevall: the road winds its way up through Wharfedale, past the amazingly intact ruins of Bolton Priory and Barden Tower. Parcevall Hall stands on the side of the fell at the top of the valley, looking out over Simon's Seat and the limestone crags, moorland and stone walls of these fine Yorkshire Dales. Once you have arrived, the only noise to be heard is the babble

of curlews. The hall is now a diocesan retreat, so this peaceful atmosphere should be observed and perpetuated. The low, stone-built house has a history that dates back to

Sadly, Parcevall Hall Gardens are not suitable for disabled visitors as some paths are steep and uneven. Notorious highwayman Will the 16th century, but it was only in 1926 that Sir William Milner (architect and horticulturist) bought Parcevall and began to create the gardens. A series of terraces falls away from the house, decorated with pools and statues and planted with surprisingly tender wall shrubs and interesting perennials. The red borders below have vast clumps of *Rheum palmatum* and other late-summer plants. The chapel garden is a shady corner of acers and hostas. The restored rose garden above provides scent and colour for much of the summer, and the rock garden is well stocked with Himalayan cowslips, candelabra primulas, gentians and much more.

The cliff walk is definitely not for the fainthearted, but it offers the most spectacular view of Troller's Ghyll. The woodland walks all around the hall are well worth exploring for beautiful camellia and rhododendron planting, not to mention the vast swathes of snowdrops, daffodils and bluebells. A programme of renovation is being carried out throughout the gardens, one area at a time.

Nevison sheltered at Parcevall, and the Barguest, a legendary black hound, howls from Troller's Ghyll.

York Gate Garden

Back Church Lane, Adel, Leeds LS16 8DW Tel 0113 2678240

Apr–Sep, Thu–Sun & BH Mon 2–5 (also Jul, Thu 6.30–9pm)

www.perennial.org.uk/yorkgate.html

This small, 0.5ha (1-acre) gem must surely have been inspired by Hidcote (*see* page 37). The Spencer family began the garden in the 1950s, and Sybil Spencer bequeathed it to Perennial (formerly the Gardeners' Royal Benevolent Society) in 1994. It is an assemblage of garden rooms, carefully organized with focal points and vistas, each a surprise. They are filled with many unusual architectural features and interesting plants. Twisted topiary and orbs of yew add structure, and paths are laid in intricate patternings of stone, gravel and cobble. The white garden, herb garden and canal all find space, as well as peony borders, seats and gazebos. Even the potting shed is nicely arranged inside, and forms part of the overall scheme of the garden. This is a truly beautifully designed garden with a sense of intimacy and peace, despite its location so close to a major city.

Note the way the pyracantha on the house is trained: it makes a horizontal green grid, stretching right across the wall.

Gresgarth Hall

Caton LA2 9NB Tel 01524 770313
Apr–Sep, 2nd Sun of every month 11–5

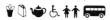

www.arabellalennoxboyd.com

Arabella Lennox-Boyd has spent two decades battling against the harsh Lancashire elements to create this superb showpiece. Ornamental woodlands and lush bog gardens merge with formal yew-hedged areas around the house. The terraces drop down to a lake, and the Artle Beck tumbles under a chinoiserie bridge. The walled kitchen garden is both picturesque and productive, with beds edged in box and wigwams of sweet

peas adding structure and height. Arabella is brilliant with colour schemes and plant associations, as evidenced in her admirable herbaceous borders, which are filled with roses, delphiniums and sweet rocket.

"If you wish to be happy your whole life long, make a garden."
Ancient Chinese proverb

Arley Hall

Arley, Northwich Cheshire CW9 6NA Tel 01565 777353
Apr–Sep, Tue–Sun & BH Mon 11–5; Oct, Sat–Sun 11–5. Last entry 4.30

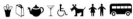

www.arleyhallandgardens.com

You enter the gardens under the half-timbered clock tower, passing between two rows of the tallest pleached limes I have ever seen. Ahead is Arley Hall, built in Victorian-Jacobean style by the Egerton-Warburtons, whose ancestors built the original hall 500 years ago. Each generation of the family (including the current owners, the Ashbrooks) has invested much love and energy in enhancing the delightful gardens. The Furlong Walk bounds the gardens along one side, separating the garden from the pretty parkland beyond. About halfway along, you come to the finest double herbaceous borders anywhere. Structural yew buttresses punctuate the long sweep of colours and a wide grass path leads up the centre to a classical summer house. The borders were originally laid out after the 'new' hall was built in 1846 and they have remained more or less unaltered.

The restaurant and shop are in the Tudor Barn, which dates back to 1469, the period of the original hall. The house (telephone for

The late Lady Elizabeth Ashbrook created the delightful Tea Cottage, which is surrounded by scented shrub roses. The Ilex Avenue is in fact holm oak (*Quercus ilex*):  great, clipped columns of them lead into the Sundial Garden, where there are lovely views across the park. From the sundial, you can wander through into The Rootree, the Victorian bog garden. You'll also find The Rough, which is planted with flowering dogwoods and other interesting shrubs.

The main walled garden has some very attractive planting sheltered by the tall brick walls. The adjacent kitchen garden produces quality fruit and vegetables and you can also admire the restored vinery.

Other little garden rooms include the Flag Garden, where many unusual tender species flourish; the Fish Garden with its reflective pool; and the Herb and Scented gardens. Take the path to the chapel and follow your nose into The Grove, an arboretum being developed by Lord Ashbrook, with plantings of rhododendrons, azaleas and other exotic trees and shrubs.

opening times) has many fine examples of plasterwork, pictures, furniture and porcelain, and a magnificent library.

Tatton Park

Knutsford, Cheshire WA16 6QN Tel 01625 534400 (switchboard) or 534435 (infoline)
Apr–Sep, Tue–Sun 10.30–6; Oct–Mar, Tue–Sun 11–4 (closed 25 Dec)

www.tattonpark.org.uk

You can have a varied day out at Tatton Park, enjoying the Home Farm, Tudor Old Hall, adventure playground and restaurant, all set in 400ha (1,000 acres) of 18th-century parkland designed by Humphry Repton. Surrounding the neoclassical mansion are glasshouses, a walled garden and a conservatory filled with exotic plants. The formality of the Italian garden is in sharp contrast to the woodlands, with its rhododendrons, azaleas and ornamental trees.

The rose gardens are overlooked by huge yew chesspiece topiary. There are herbaceous borders, pergolas, pools and a maze. The jewel in Tatton's crown is the peaceful Japanese tea garden, at its best in autumn, when the acers turn to colours of fire.

At the Home Farm your family can see all of the customary farm animals and take part in events such as pig washing and egg painting

Renishaw Hall Gardens

Renishaw, near Sheffield S21 3WB Tel 01246 432310

Apr–Sep, Thu–Sun & BH 10.30–4.30

www.sitwell.co.uk

Renishaw Hall has looked out from the top of a Derbyshire hill since the 17th century, but the gardens we see today were born later, created by Sir George Sitwell between 1886 and 1936. A series of terraces with lawns, precision-cut yew hedges, and classical statues, urns, ponds and fountains form the backbone of the fine formal, Italianate gardens. These are enhanced by voluptuous mixed borders in carefully selected colour schemes. The terrace walls support roses, clematis, wisteria and

jasmine. In the bluebell woods a path flanked by pink camellias leads to the classical temple and a young woodland garden. There are walks around the lakes, and an orangery houses the National Collection of Yuccas.

A number of modern sculptures are exhibited within the grounds, and remarkable collection of John Piper's work is on view in the gallery.

Chatsworth

Bakewell, Derbyshire DE45 1PP Tel 01246 565300
Jun–Aug, daily 10.30–6; Apr–May & Sep–Dec, daily 11–6

www.chatsworth.org

The earliest reference to a garden at Chatsworth was in 1560. Towards the end of the 17th century the 1st Duke of Devonshire replaced the original house and laid out vast, formal gardens and terraces to complement the impressive building.

Some 60 years later the 4th Duke of Devonshire employed Lancelot 'Capability' Brown to landscape the park and gardens. The formal gardens, with a few exceptions, were replaced by the English Landscape parkland through which you approach the house today.

Joseph Paxton was appointed head gardener in the early part of the 19th century and it was he created who the vast rockery and the Great Conservatory – a greenhouse of monumental size which, sadly, was demolished in the 1920s. Its foundations are still visible, and a maze has been constructed within

Allow at least two hours to look round the house, which is filled with a breathtaking collection of pictures, statues, and *objets d'ar*

them. In 1844 Paxton modelled the Emperor Fountain, named after Tsar Nicholas I, Emperor of Russia. The fountain comprises a gravity-fed jet that plays almost 90m (300ft) high – a true masterpiece of engineering.

There is so much to see, you need to buy the guidebook to make sure that you don't miss anything. See for yourselves the exquisite vistas and avenues, the Ring Pond and Serpentine Walk, the kitchen garden, the pinetum, the rose garden, the grotto, the dazzling cascade, the Conservative Wall glasshouse and the Willow Tree Fountain (which so delighted the young Queen Victoria).

For the past 50 years the current inhabitants of Chatsworth, the 11th Duke and Duchess, have continued to enhance both the house and grounds. Additions include *Revelation*, a dramatic water-powered sculpture by Angela Connor situated on one of the oldest ponds in the gardens; Elisabeth Frink's *Walking Madonna*; the Cottage Garden, and much more.

he restaurant and shops in the house and stables are top-quality.
isit the farm shop (signed on way out) for Chatsworth produce.

NOTTINGHAMSHIRE■NEAR NEWARK

Pureland Japanese Garden

North Clifton, Newark, Nottinghamshire NG23 7AT Tel 01777 228567
Apr–Oct, Tue–Fri 10.30–5.30, Sat–Sun & BH 10–5.30 (also Aug–Sep, Fri–Sun 7–10pm, by lantern light)

www.jaz93.demon.co.uk/purelands.htm

It is somewhat curious to park behind a barn in a Nottinghamshire village and emerge the other side to find the courteous Japanese garden creator, Buddha Maitreya, clad in apricot robes and bowing in welcome. By taking the traditional elements of a Japanese garden and adding his own embellishments, Maitreya has created a peaceful haven to complement his meditation centre. Winding, narrow paths take you across ponds and over trickling streams, passing pagodas and lanterns. Large, colourful clumps

of perennials add an excellent contrast to the clipped cloud-shaped conifers and Japanese maples. The soft singing of wind chimes accompanies you all the way.

Hodsock Priory near Worksop (tel 01909 591204) is worth a visit i early spring for the beautiful 'Snowdrop Spectacular'.

Barnsdale Gardens

The Avenue, Exton, Oakham, Rutland LE15 8AH Tel 01572 813200

Jun–Aug daily 9–7; Mar–May, Sep–Oct 9–5; Nov–Feb 10–4. Last entry 2 hours before close

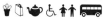

www.barnsdalegardens.co.uk

The late Geoff Hamilton presented BBC TV's *Gardeners' World* for many years, winning a place in many people's hearts with his easy manner, inventive ideas and immense knowledge. Barnsdale was the garden where he put his ideas into practice, and you'll find many familiar corners. There are cottage gardens, town gardens, herb and vegetable gardens, Mediterranean and Japanese gardens, ponds, rockeries, rose beds, winter borders and so much more, all beautifully maintained. Geoff would

have loved to see how well his creations have matured. So, if you used to look forward to watching him every Friday, come to Barnsdale. It's like meeting up with an old friend.

Geoff's son and daughter-in-law are now at the helm, and there is an excellent nursery to visit and some new borders and gardens.

Wollerton Old Hall Garden

Wollerton, Market Drayton, Shropshire TF9 3NA Tel 01630 685760

Easter–Aug, Fri, Sun & BH, noon–5; Sep, Sun, noon–5

www.wollertonoldhallgarden.com

John and Lesley Jenkins have spent 20 years creating a garden of contrasts hidden alluringly behind this majestic 500-year-old hall (unfortunately not open to the public).

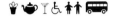

Market Drayton ▲

Wollerton Old Hall

Wollerton

A53

A stone path leads you from the front of the house through to a series of hedged enclosures. You pass topiary, scented rose beds, areas for spring bulbs and herbaceous planting with towering delphiniums, before arriving in the Croft Garden – a miniature informal woodland that has unusual trees and shrubs and an untamed feel.

Within the main garden, opulent scented borders and rose arches open out into simply furnished spaces. The secluded Well Garden's centrepiece is a limestone well-head surrounded by pyramid

Nearby Hodnet Hall has charming gardens that include a series o beautifully planted informal lakes. There is also a very fine peon

yews. It is planted with
the palest tints of white,
cream and yellow. After
the volcanic colours in
the Lanhydrock Garden,
(named after the famous
Cornish garden), the

pleached lime allée is cool and green. The main herbaceous
border is redolent of Jekyll, with its diagonal drifts and
graduated colours from white and lemon through apricot,
pink and plum to violet and blue. It leads you to the Rill
Garden with its cool, reflective, formal pond and gazebo
adorned with honeysuckle and 'Champney's Pink Cluster'
roses. The shade garden – a dry area underneath silver birches –
is full of ideas to take home for that gloomy, dry, awkward
space. There are many interesting foliage plants including
ferns and hostas, and there's winter and spring interest from
hellebores, trilliums, meconopsis and all manner of bulbs.
Wollerton Old Hall Garden is inspirational. It is beautiful,
elegant, classical yet modern and full of unusual and
interesting plants. It is a credit to the Jenkins' hard work and
imagination and is a genuine delight to visit.

border, a kitchen garden and woodland walks with ericaceous
trees and shrubs (tel 01630 685202).

Packwood House

Lapworth, Solihull B94 6AT Tel 01564 783294
May–Sep, Wed–Sun & BH Mon 11–5.30; Oct 11–4.30; Mar–Apr 11–4.30

www.nationaltrust.org.uk

This 16th-century house is situated in the Forest of Arden. As you arrive you step back in time, forgetting the urban sprawl just a few miles away. There is a Carolean walled courtyard with corner gazebos, and a wonderful sunken garden with a pool. The herbaceous borders are imaginatively planted and full of colour; in late summer red-hot pokers rocket forth among silver foliage. The most striking feature is the unique Yew

Garden – vast, tapered columns, are said to represent the Sermon on the Mount: the 12 apostles (the tallest yews) are surrounded by a smaller multitude, and a path spirals up the mound at end of the garden to 'The Preacher'.

The head gardener leads guided walks on occasional summer evenings. Open-air theatre productions are also staged here.

The Dorothy Clive Garden

Willoughbridge, Market Drayton, Shropshire TF9 4EU Tel 01630 647237
Mid-Mar to mid-Nov, daily 10–5.30

www.dorothyclivegarden.co.uk

Colonel Harry Clive created the gardens as a place of beauty for his wife, Dorothy, to enjoy as her health deteriorated in the final years of her life. After her death in 1942 he developed them further as a memorial. The old quarry at the top of the garden, with mature oaks overhead, is a perfect site for woodland shrubs and small trees. Spring bulbs carpet the area and bog plants hug the banks of the stepped waterfall. Nearby is the Secret Garden, with a long pool and rockeries. Further down the hill in huge, sunny, informal beds are shrubs, roses, dwarf conifers, massed perennials, annuals and bulbs. Specimen trees add height and structure, and there are lovely views over the countryside. At the bottom of the hill alpine scree beds surround a pool, planted with marginal and aquatic perennials. This is a vast horticultural treasure trove, with many rare and unusual plants.

The labelling is excellent, the staff are helpful, and there is a good tea room with lovely views of the gardens.

Biddulph Grange

Grange Road, Biddulph, Stoke-on-Trent ST8 7SD Tel 01782 517999
Apr–Oct, Wed–Fri 12–5.30, Sat–Sun & BH Mon 11–5.30 (or dusk); Nov–Dec, Sat–Sun 12–4

www.nationaltrust.org.uk

Biddulph Grange is an extraordinarily fine example of a Victorian garden, both in layout and planting, and it is also a garden of many surprises. Crammed into its 6ha (15 acres) is a bizarre and eclectic selection of formal and informal realms, decorated with peerless statues and garden buildings, ponds, rockeries, tunnels and more. The formal terraces around the house drop away to a lake fringed

with rhododendrons and azaleas. An archway through the surrounding rockery takes you to the woodland garden and features such as the Quoit Ground and the Bowling Green. Another dark tunnel – just long enough to make you feel quite apprehensive – leads you into 'China',

Typical Victorian planting included evergreens such as conifers, hollies, monkey puzzle trees, laurels, yews and gaultheria. Border

130

as you emerge into a brightly painted Chinese temple. Through its fretted windows you view a secret garden with maples, peonies, ferns and pines, all reflected in a pond with a bridge and a golden buffalo. Passing through the Cheshire Cottage you find 'Egypt', with its stone Sphinx and yew pyramids. There is also an Italian garden, an arboretum, a lime avenue and the Wellingtonia Avenue, which was replanted in 1976 (we'll have to wait a century to see it fully mature). You'll also find a pinetum, a stumpery (upside-down tree-stumps for growing ferns – a passion of the Victorians), rose gardens, the dahlia borders, parterres and more.

These are the eccentric fancies of James and Maria Bateman, who conceived and realized this remarkable creation in the mid-19th century. The garden was neglected after the 1920s and became totally overgrown, but its restoration

(undertaken since 1988 by the National Trust) has been a historical and horticultural success story, and Biddulph continues to be developed with empathy and care.

were laid out in formal patterns and incorporated tender bedding plants. Visit the dahlia borders in late summer to see such a scheme.

"God Almighty first planted a garden; indeed it is the purest of human pleasures."

Francis Bacon (1561–1626)

Wales

Bodnant

Tal y Cafn, near Colwyn Bay, Conwy, Wales LL28 5RE Tel 01492 650460

Mid-Mar to Oct, daily 10–5. Last entry 4

www.bodnantgarden.co.uk

Bodnant sits on the south-facing, wooded slope of the Conwy valley in North Wales. Surrounding the 19th-century house are large lawns and trees. There are rose beds, herbaceous borders and a very famous pergola that drips with golden laburnum flowers

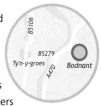

in late May. The lawns fall away from the house in a series of formal, Italianate terraces with ponds, yew hedges, borders and topiary. These are stunning: they are beautifully planted, and well maintained. The view across to the hills of Snowdonia

is breathtaking. Also superb is the much-photographed Pin Mill, which stands at the end of the reflective canal. As you leave these sunny spaces you drop into a cool,

The Pin Mill was originally built in 1730 as a garden house i Gloucestershire. It was later used as a mill for the manufacture o

green, cathedral-like valley; its pillars are vast conifers and its congregation is formed by camellias, azaleas, rhododendrons, and a diverse collection of  woodland shrubs. Giant magnolias battle towards the canopy, hydrangeas provide late-summer colour and Japanese maples turn to shades of flame in autumn. The stream trickling through The Dell is planted with astilbes, primulas, skunk cabbage and other waterside plants.

Many famous collectors have contributed to the woodland plantings commissioned by the 2nd Lord Aberconwy at the end of the 19th century and continued by successive generations. These include E H Wilson, George Forrest and Frank Kingdon-Ward, who all sent species back from China and the Himalayas that have thrived here. Many new cultivars raised at Bodnant bear the name of the garden.

The Aberconwy family still lives in the house and manages the grounds for the National Trust, ensuring the continued enhancement of this important and historic garden.

ɔins, and then as a tannery. It fell into disrepair before being ɔrought to Bodnant to be rebuilt in 1939.

Powis Castle

Welshpool SY21 8RF Tel 01938 551920
Apr–Oct, Wed–Sun 11–6 (also Jul–Aug, Tue)

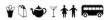

www.nationaltrust.org.uk

The day I visited Powis Castle the skies were cobalt blue and the distant hills shimmered in the heat. It was a magical day and a wondrous place, justifiably one of the nation's favourite gardens.

The steeply terraced, 17th-century, Italianate gardens cling to the petticoats of the imposing castle. They escaped the axe of the Landscape Movement in the 18th

century for lack of any alternatives, and are, as a result, historic and astonishing. Giant, cloud-shaped, ancient yews dominate the top terrace (I would hate to be in charge of hedge cutting here!), and a group of yuccas in the rockery adds an exotic feel. On the aviary terrace below stand the famous lead figures of shepherds and shepherdesses in front of a

Welsh princes built the castle in 13th century, and it was subsequently owned by the Herbert and Clive families. There is

curtain of wisteria, flanked by borders of Mediterranean planting. The orangery terrace is dazzlingly colourful: reds, royal blues and yellows jostle for space in box-edged borders – the brilliance of the colours works wonders in this precipitous situation. The terraces accommodate a vast range of plants, such as roses, clematis, shrubs and perennials including acca, iochroma, olearia, arbutus, isoplexis, and veratrum. They are cleverly planted and immaculately kept. Despite cold winters, many tender species grow successfully here, warmed by the night-store heat of the terrace walls. With its vast array of unusual plants, this is a garden to be enjoyed by both the amateur and the expert horticulturalist. Formal gardens lie below the terraces and incorporate fruit trees and ground-cover plants. Beyond the daffodil meadows are woodland gardens from which you gain fine views back to the castle.

Spend the whole day at Powis. A quick visit would not be enough for you to soak up the magic and history, and to appreciate the expert, artful planting.

Glansevern Hall Gardens

Berriew, Welshpool, Powys SY21 8AH Tel 01686 640200
May–Sep, Fri–Sat & BH Mon, noon–6

www.glansevern.co.uk

This friendly, family-run garden is a joy to visit. The dominant feature is the large lily-strewn lake with its good collection of unusual ornamental trees. Adjacent is a well-planted water garden, lush with a profusion of bog-loving perennials. The Greek Revival house (c1800) has formal rosebeds, flower borders and views over the Folly Garden and across parkland to the River Severn. Passing the Victorian rock garden and grotto, you enter the *pièce de résistance*: a series of formal schemes within the

walled garden, flourishing with colour and scent. This is a romantic place of secret corners. You will find the shop and tea room (try the Welsh cakes) in the attractive stables courtyard.

The tree collection includes specimens of the nettle tree, the dove tree, the cucumber tree and the foxglove tree.

Aberglasney Gardens

Llangathen, Carmarthenshire SA32 8QH Tel 01558 668998
Apr–Oct, daily 10–6. Last entry 5; Nov–Mar 10.30–4 (closed 25 Dec)

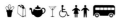

www.aberglasney.org

The moment you arrive at Aberglasney you'll understand why I have included this small, ancient garden. Enter this lovely, peaceful place and you step back in time. The 17th-century cloister garden has a simple pattern of lawn shapes which, in early May,

sprout the favourite flower of the Ottoman empire – the elegant acuminate tulip. There is a kitchen garden and another walled area with borders designed by Penelope Hobhouse. The woodlands have been planted with boggy shade-lovers such

as trilliums, hostas and primulas. Seeing Aberglasney in the throes of its restoration is exciting – visit regularly. The gardens are well maintained, with good facilities and pleasant staff.

The plant centre and shop are very good quality, and the guidebook has some excellent plant photography within its pages.

Dyffryn Gardens

St Nicholas, near Cardiff, Vale of Glamorgan CF5 6SU Tel 02920 593328
Apr–Sep, daily 10–6; Oct 10–5; Nov–Mar 10–4

www.dyffryngardens.org.uk

John Cory built the present house at Dyffryn in 1893 and commissioned the landscape architect Thomas Mawson to design the gardens. Cory's son, Reginald, a keen plantsman, further embellished the 22ha (55 acres) in the early 1900s. With help from the Heritage Lottery Fund's £6.15 million grant, the present owners (Vale of Glamorgan Council) are restoring Dyffryn

to its full Edwardian glory. Notable features include an arboretum, a Victorian fernery, a precipitous rockery, formal bedding schemes, a long central canal and some unusual statues, which have been restored and returned to

Clyne Gardens near Swansea comprise 20ha (50 acres) of outstanding woodland gardens, with internationally renowned

their original positions. Not far from the current restoration project (the walled garden), and surrounded by elegant, sweeping lawns, is a series of small, yew-hedged rooms, each with its own character. These

rooms include a physic garden, a rose garden, a pool garden and the faithfully resurrected Pompeiian Garden, which captures the flavour of ancient Italy. The 100m-long (330ft) double herbaceous borders are extremely well planted.

Dyffryn's remarkable arboretum contains many rare species and boasts 15 'champion trees' – the tallest or largest of their varieties in the UK. Don't miss the spectacular winter illuminations, when the magnificent trees are lit up with magical effects (phone to check opening times).

This is a place where the faded glory of a bygone era is wonderfully being brought back to its former eminence. There is a tea room serving light refreshments and a shop that sells a variety of plants and other horticultural items.

collections of rhododendrons, pieris and enkianthus, many interesting trees and a varied bog garden (tel 01792 401737).

"Nature has the will but not the power to realize perfection."

Aristotle (384–322 BC)

Scotland

The Castle of Mey

Thurso, Caithness, Highland KW14 8XH Tel 01847 851473
Mid-May to Jul, Tue–Sat 11–4.30; mid-Aug to Sep, Sun 2–5

www.castleofmey.org.uk

This 16th-century castle was one of the late Queen Mother's favourite homes: she visited twice a year. It stands by the sea on the very north coast of Scotland – a bleak, windswept place where tough native trees struggle to grow straight. It is the high stone wall (the Great Wall of Mey) that enables a garden to exist here at all. Old-fashioned roses, dahlias and bedding plants bring

colour; fruit and vegetables are grown for the house, and perennial borders flourish. The garden reflects the Queen Mother's preferences: some plants were gifts and others were simply her favourites. She was a knowledgeable, keen gardener, as is apparent in this delightful, intimate place.

The Scottish Thistle is thought to be *Cirsium vulgare*, or Spear Thistle. A white-flowered form can be found on Orkney.

Inverewe Garden

Poolewe, Ross-shire, Highland IV22 2LG Tel 01445 781200
Apr–Oct, daily 9.30–9 or dusk; Nov–Mar 9.30–4

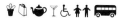

www.nts.org.uk

Violent gales and salt-laden winds are the drawbacks of gardening on Scotland's northwest coast. In 1862 Osgood Mackenzie built the house and planted shelterbelt woodlands. He walled a curved, sloping area and imported soil mixed with seaweed, enabling him to grow fruit, vegetables, herbs and flowers. The woods are planted with a diverse, extensive collection of large-leaved rhododendrons and flowering shrubs, and many paths afford stunning views of the sea loch and mountains beyond. In the wooded valleys are streams and pools exquisitely adorned with

drifts of meconopsis and candelabra primulas. Herbaceous borders and a rock garden surround the house. Inverewe is a marvellous garden, worthy of a long diversion.

The midges are famously vicious and sometimes prolific. Either visit before mid-May, or remember to bring your anti-midge cream!

Drummond Castle Gardens

Muthill, Crieff, Perth and Kinross PH5 2AA Tel 01764 681257
Easter, open 4 days 1–6; May–Oct, daily 1–6. Last entry 5

www.drummondcastlegardens.co.uk

The castle, dating from 1490, stands tall above Scotland's finest formal gardens. Originally laid out in the early 17th century, the gardens were remodelled in the mid-1800s by Lewis Kennedy. The enormous parterre based on St Andrew's cross comprises marble statues, fountains and urns; topiary and neatly clipped trees; roses, colourful herbaceous planting and beds brimming with brilliant bedding plants. The central feature is a sundial made by Charles I's stonemason. Architecture and colour work together in this exuberant, visionary arrangement. The central

axis of the parterre runs from the castle to the kitchen garden beyond, through woodland, and away into the distance.

Look for the copper beech tree planted by Queen Victoria when she visited the 'very fine' gardens at Drummond Castle in 1842.

House of Pitmuies

by Forfar, Angus DD8 2SN Tel 01241 828245
Mid-Apr to Oct, daily 10–5

www.pitmuies.com

Brechin ▲

A932 House of Pitmuies

A961 A933

Arbroath ▼

The house at Pitmuies dates from 1730 and looks onto a much younger garden that perfectly complements the house and the surrounding Angus countryside (where you can enjoy riverside walks). Old fruit trees enhance the potager with its themed borders: a bed for tender plants, one for foliage plants and so on. There are climbing roses, honeysuckle and flowers for cutting, all within old stone walls. Around the house are spectacular plantings in formal schemes. The summer borders, backed by dark red

prunus hedges, are filled with blue, white and pink perennials; and the rose gardens contain many different varieties. The most notable features of this lovely place are the delphiniums: there is something magical about their fine, towering, blue spires.

In the 1930s New York florist Max Schling said "The love of flowers is really the best teacher of how to grow and understand them".

Arduaine Garden

Arduaine, Oban, Argyll PA34 4XQ Tel 01852 2003666
Daily 9.30–dusk

www.nts.org.uk

To the west of Arduaine (pronounced Ardoony) there is only a clutch of islands before the coast of Labrador, yet this green, wooded peninsula has a mild (if windy) climate and is far from bleak. A century ago the house, garden and, most importantly, the shelterbelts were put in place by J Arthur Campbell, a wealthy tea merchant and diamond prospector. By the late 1920s the woodland gardens already held 220 types of rhododendron, –

and this is what Arduaine is famous for – but there are other interesting and often tender plants to enjoy in this picturesque place. Ponds, bogs, rockeries, an alpine meadow and matchless views over Loch Melfort make this a very special garden.

Ardmaddy Castle near Balvicar (open daily 9–dusk) has sea views and a well-planted walled garden (tel 01852 300353).

Mount Stuart

Isle of Bute PA20 9LR Tel 01700 503877

May–Sep, Fri–Mon & Wed 10–6; Apr & Oct, some weekends

www.mountstuart.com

The vast, eccentric, gothic mansion replaced an earlier house destroyed by fire in 1877. The grounds cover 120ha (300 acres), which have been developed over three centuries. Well-marked walks take you along tree-lined avenues and through the mature pinetum and rock garden with its cascades and pools. The 'Wee Garden' (2ha/ 5 acres!) contains a superb collection of southern hemisphere shrubs. The kitchen garden, designed by Rosemary Verey and adapted by James Alexander-Sinclair, has a central glass pavilion surrounded by herbaceous beds. The walls support trained fruit trees; there are beds of culinary and medicinal herbs, and a large orchard. Mount Stuart has walks with sea views, picnic areas, an ultra-modern visitor centre, an adventure playground and a great deal more to enjoy. Take time to look round the house: the wildly lavish interior cannot fail to impress!

A 40ha (100-acre) pinetum has been planted, with species from 13 different countries, as part of the Conifer Conservation Programme.

Little Sparta

Stonypath, Dunsyre, Lanark ML11 8NG Tel 01899 810252
Mid-Jun to Sep, Fri & Sun 2–5

www.gardens-guide.com

Garden: 'a piece of ground used for growing flowers...a place of recreation...ornamental grounds laid out for public enjoyment...'
So reads the dictionary definition, and I wanted to check it because Little Sparta is not like any other garden. It is, however, a work of great artistic importance and, indeed, a place of enjoyment and recreation. Ian Hamilton Finlay is a poet and sculptor, and this bleak, wild place in the Pentland hills is his vision and passion. Blocks of stone carved with inscriptions are carefully placed near small lochs or built into walls, and verses from Virgil are inscribed in circles of granite. There are signs, symbols and messages to be found everywhere: even the choice of trees has meaning. You must explore, read, puzzle and ponder. It is an emotional and marvellous place. Yes, a garden, and one of the most inspired and original to be found.

Visit Broughton Place near Biggar for a complete contrast: a floriferous, traditional garden that is just lovely (tel 01899 830234).

Crathes Castle

Banchory, Aberdeenshire AB31 5QJ Tel 01330 844525
Daily 9–dusk

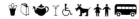

www.nts.org.uk

This 16th-century bulding is the very epitome of what one expects from a Scottish castle: gargoyles, turrets and battlements. The walled garden would originally have been an important provider of food for the household. Over the centuries it has developed into eight ornamental rooms, some bounded by fine yew hedges. The colours are carefully controlled – you enter through the scented shrubs and silver foliage of the famous white borders. Beyond are beds of soft blues and pinks, a golden garden and spectacular June borders planted with shades of cerise, scarlet and violet, with delightful views of the stone 'doocot' (or dovecote). Beyond the walls there are mature woodlands with nature trails to enjoy.

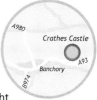

The Burnett family built Crathes and lived there for over 400 years until 1951, when it was given to the Scottish National Trust.

Manderston

Duns, Borders TD11 3PP Tel 01361 883450
Mid-May to Sep, Thu, Sun & BH 2–dusk

www.manderston.co.uk

Manderston embodies the essence of Edwardian grand style. It is a Georgian family seat remodelled in a neo-Georgian style at the turn of the last century by Sir James Miller, to honour his new wife (and to impress his father-in-law, Lord Scarsdale).

Near to the house are wide, balustraded terraces designed by architect John Kinross. They are decorated with fountains and formal beds filled with brightly coloured roses, hostas and

gold and green topiary. Imposing gilded gates lead to the formal gardens and their glowing bedding schemes, rose pergola, fountains and statuary. From the terraces you get

The early 18th-century Mertoun (near St Boswells) is one of the prettiest houses on the River Tweed. Its grounds include a very a wonderful view over the serpentine lake and chinoiserie bridge to the landscaped woods and parkland, all dating from the 18th century. In the distance you can see the rolling Cheviot Hills: this must be one of the finest outlooks of any house. The woodland garden (best seen in late May or June) has been constantly enhanced since Sir James's day and is now home to an excellent collection of pieris, azalea and rhododendron (over 180 species) and some unusual trees. Manderston's 23ha (56 acres) really are magnificent: Lord Scarsdale certainly must have been impressed!

fine kitchen garden, beautiful herbaceous borders, an arboretum and lawns sweeping down to the river (tel 01835 823236).

Logan Botanic Garden

Port Logan, Stranraer, Dumfries and Galloway DG9 9ND Tel 01776 860231

Apr–Sep, daily 10–6; Oct 10–5; Mar 10–5

www.rbge.org.uk

This is one of Scotland's four national botanic gardens. All have important, varied collections and are well worth visiting. Edinburgh's Royal Botanic Garden boasts a famous rock garden, 10 glasshouses, woodland, heath and peat gardens. The Benmore Botanic Gardens and the Dawyck Botanic Gardens in the Borders grow trees, rhododendrons and other flowering shrubs. But Logan is different. Despite being surrounded by sea on three sides

(and so occasionally attacked by salt-laden gales), it is warmed and regularly watered by the Gulf Stream, which permits it to grow a huge range of tender and exotic plants. This is a plantsman's paradise, with 2,300

The evergreen shrub *Drimys winteri* or 'Winter's Bark' is from the Andes and is named after Captain William Winter, who sailed with

taxa from all temperate areas of the globe, nearly half of which are of wild origin. Their existence at Logan ensures that they are sustained in cultivation – a crucial factor when so many species are threatened with extinction in their natural habitats.

However, Logan is also simply a beautiful place to visit, full of vivid colours and exotic shapes. Towering palms and tree ferns stand cheek by jowl with silvery gum trees. Swathes of salvias, fuchsias, felicias, verbenas and argyranthemums provide a range of brilliant summer colour, and South American bog and pond plants add a tropical note. Bottle brushes and cabbage palms from the Antipodes flower profusely, as do clianthus, sophora, crinodendron, embothrium and acacia. Magnolias and camellias are out in the early part of the year, and pink, scented crinums blossom in late summer. Keep an eye open for the remarkable

giant Himalayan lilies, *Cardiocrinum giganteum*. Another curious sight is the drifts of daffodils that bloom under the avenue of Chusan palms. Logan is a wonderful, important and educational garden.

rancis Drake in 1578. Winter treated the sailors' scurvy with this romatic bark, which contains high levels of vitamin C.

155

Index

Page numbers are shown in **bold**.

Acknowledgements

Veronica Mackinnon would like to thank all the staff at Studio Cactus for their hard work and good humour, especially Damien Moore and Mandy Lunn for the opportunity; Laura Watson for stylish design; Sue Gordon and Emily Hawkins for expert editing; and Aaron Brown for his enthusiastic input. Thanks to Pussy and Bella for five-star accommodation; to Mum for the reason I am a gardener; to Caroline, Nick, Rich and Chris for inspiration and laughs; and to Berts, Lucy and Angus for so much love and a fine life.

Studio Cactus would like to thank Claire Moore for creating the maps.

Picture Credits
All photography by Veronica Mackinnon with the exception of the following:
Corbis: 11; Cranborne Manor: 79; Trewithen: 97; Tresco Abbey: 98, 99; The Castle of Mey: 144; Inverewe Garden: 145; Kathy Collins: 146; House of Pitmuies: 147; Crathes Castle: 151; Manderston: 152, 153; Logan Botanic Garden: 154, 155.

Also in this series...

Tip-top Teashops
The indispensable guide
to a great British tradition

Tip-top Fish & Chip Shops
The indispensable guide to
Britain's favourite fast food

"Fascinating...crammed full
of information, including
location maps, opening
hours, and local specialities."

Daily Express

Tip-top

TEASHOPS

Laura Harper